A WRITER'S GUIDE TO RESEARCH

A WRITER'S GUIDE TO RESEARCH

Lois Horowitz

Cincinnati, Ohio

To my mother

Library of Congress Cataloging in Publication Data

Horowitz, Lois
    A writer's guide to research.

    Includes index.
    1. Authorship—Handbooks, manuals, etc. 2. Research—Handbooks, manuals, etc. I. Title.
PN146.H67   1986   001.4   86-4052
ISBN 0-89879-222-3

PERMISSION ACKNOWLEDGMENTS

Grateful acknowledgment is made for permission to reprint excerpts from the following:

CIS/Index and Abstracts to Publications of the U.S. Congress, 1980 issue, published by Congressional Information Service, Inc.

CIS U.S. Congressional Committee Hearings Index, 1969 issue, published by Congressional Information Service, Inc.

CIS U.S. Congressional Committee Prints Index, published by Congressional Information Service, Inc.

CIS U.S. Serial Set Index, 1857-79 issue, published by Congressional Information Service, Inc.

Cumulative Subject Index to the Monthly Catalog of United States Government Publications, 1900-71, published by Carrollton Press.

Cumulative Title Index to United States Public Documents, 1789-1976, published by United States Historical Documents Institute.

Index to U.S. Government Periodicals, 1980-81 issues, published by Infordata International, Inc.

Magazine Index, 1979-84 microfilm edition, published by Information Access Corp.

Public Affairs Information Service Bulletin, 1980 issue, published by Public Affairs Information Service, Inc.

Statistical Reference Index, 1981 issue, published by Congressional Information Service, Inc.

Subject Guide to Books in Print, 1978/79, 1982/83 issues, published by R.R. Bowker & Co.

Writings on American History, 1935 issue, published by the American Historical Association.

ACKNOWLEDGMENTS

I would like to thank the staff of Writer's Digest Books, Carol Cartaino, Nan Dibble, John Andraud, and others, for their efficiency and cooperation in working on this research guide for writers. It proves that people with common goals can work well together even if they have never met.

CONTENTS

PREFACE

There are two important things a writer must have to earn a living in this field. They are a word processor and solid research skills. Both have the amazing facility to free your valuable time for the activity you want to do most—write.

Many words have been written about writer's block. I have never experienced it. In fact, I don't believe it exists. For me, writer's block has always been either fatigue or a less commonly known affliction I call researcher's block.

Screenwriter Lawrence Kasdan once said that being a writer is like having homework the rest of your life. For many of us, our school years epitomized researcher's block disguising itself as writer's block. It's not the hand that writes; it's the mind. Once you incorporate the research pattern into your writing life, you may discover yourself miraculously cured of writer's block.

I recall a friend, children's writer Karen O'Connor, telling me that a nonfiction young adult book had taken her seven months—six months to research and one month to write. "After the research," she said, "the writing flowed."

Few beginning writers realize that writing starts not with a pencil, typewriter, or word processor. It starts with research. When that is done, your writing can't help but flow.

—Lois Horowitz

1
WHERE IS INFORMATION?

I'm a stickler for research.

That's what magazine editor Dick Harris once told me. He wasn't the first to say it, nor are magazine editors the only editors concerned with research.

Book editors are just as particular, and with good reason. Carelessly researched books can be legal liabilities. Poorly researched books seldom reach print.

At a writers' conference held in San Diego, book editor Patricia Golbitz told a group of writers how she evaluates nonfiction book proposals: "The first thing I ask about an author is, 'What are your credentials? How are you qualified to write this book?' "

Writers don't need a doctorate to succeed. Many writers earn their credentials by specializing in a subject and learning everything they can about it. They prove themselves through their knowledge and their research ability. A major concern to all writers is how to do research quickly and efficiently.

WHERE IS INFORMATION?

Information is everywhere—in books and newspapers, even in death certificates and on billboards. To tap the right source, you must know the differences among the various information providers.

Libraries are the major keepers of information but by no means the only ones. Museums, television stations, manufacturers, and governmental agencies, among others, also store information.

These providers not only differ by category, but individual providers also differ from others of their kind. All libraries do not buy the same books and magazines. Museums focus on interests from Greek antiquities to locomotives. Companies research and produce anything from auto seat belts to dried foods.

Following is a brief look at some information outlets and what each has to offer.

Public libraries

Most of us start our research at the public library. Be aware, however, that one public library may be a very different beast from another nearby. They may differ in size, budget, and staffing, and hence in service.

Your first stop may be the neighborhood branch of your city's library system. Branches usually own *Reader's Guide to Periodical Literature* and perhaps a few other indexes to magazines. Maybe they maintain small collections of reference books—encyclopedias, dictionaries, and quotation books—or allow their magazines to circulate.

Branches can often serve as links between you and other libraries. Through such branches, you can order, pick up and drop off reserve books and interlibrary-loan materials. They may also have computer and microfilm catalogs for other libraries in your region, so that you can see what those libraries own without having to visit or call each one.

Some branch libraries give away donated material and have regular book sales—excellent sources for finding new magazine markets and inexpensive reference books.

Many large public libraries or a library system's main branch will be well equipped to handle more challenging and complicated research problems. They may not, however, always be appropriate for every type of writing project. For such projects, you may need to consult a special library.

Academic libraries

Academic libraries intimidate many writers. A number of these libraries, however, *are* open to the public. Though service to "outsiders" may be limited, some sell annual-fee cards to let you check out books. And most will let you come in and use the collection without a card or identification.

Eventually you'll use academic libraries. They simply have more (and different) materials than most public libraries. They buy out-of-print as well as current books, technical as well as popular, foreign as well as American-published material. Historical novelists will find more reprinted diaries and old books; medical writers, more technical health reports, at academic libraries than at public libraries.

To determine the subject strengths of the library (and bookstore) at a college or university, check the school's major courses of study through the catalog. You'll usually find catalogs at public libraries (and at the institutions themselves). For example, Columbia University is known for its majors in journalism and Italian literature; Bowling Green (Ohio) State University has strong programs in philosophy and popular culture. To support those majors, they must have exceptional library collections in those fields. Conversely, if a school offers no degree in education, its library collection in education will be inadequate.

Community college libraries

Many community colleges train students in the trades. Therefore, their libraries and bookstores buy texts in such fields as brick masonry, food service, locksmithing, travel-agency management, auto and aircraft mechanics, and carpentry. Like academic libraries, many community colleges offer free, in-house use of their libraries, and cards for a fee.

An advantage of using college libraries is that they're usually open on weekends and late at night, a boon to writers who work during the day. Hours frequently change according to seasons, terms, and final-exam schedules, so call before you visit.

Historical society libraries

Historical societies vary in size and sophistication; their staffs range from volunteers with little research experience to specially trained archivists.

Their collections focus on the history of their region, and they usually own material available nowhere else—prisoner-of-war diaries kept by local vets, old photos of the area, local archaeological records, minutes and membership roll books of defunct organizations, family histories, and more.

Call ahead for the society's hours. Some also charge a library-user's fee for non-society members. If you're starting a long-term project and will make extended use of the library, consider joining for the year. Fees are usually reasonable and tax deductible.

Museum libraries

Museum libraries usually parallel the subject of the museum's collection, whether it's regional wildlife or gemstones. Most museum curators are specialists in their fields, and large museums maintain special libraries to support their research. The collection of the New York Museum of Transportation in West Henrietta, New York, for example, focuses on transportation patterns used in the area between 1880 and 1955. It also has a six thousand-volume library, maps, photos, articles, and technical data.

Some museum libraries are only open to the staff or members, but depending on their size, staff, and budget, they still may handle mail or phone queries. Rules of operation and use vary, but generally the larger the museum, the better its library and public service.

Company libraries

Large companies such as Goodyear Tire and Rubber, the Chase Manhattan Bank, and Rockwell International have extensive staff libraries and may not handle many requests for information from the public.

If a company specializes in your subject (gasless engines or new arthritis drugs, for example), write or call anyway. If they can't give you specific information, they may refer you to experts or send you copies of articles and reports covering their research.

Information about a company and its product or service is usually available through its public-relations office. Sometimes this office will circumvent restricted library access and get information for you that you can't get yourself.

Special collections and special libraries

Most public and academic libraries have separate rooms called special collections departments, which house the rare and unique material the library cannot accommodate in its regular collection. Items may include rare first editions, hand-lettered (illuminated) manuscripts, broadsides (posters), miniature books; even sculpture, ancient scrolls, coins, paintings, and antique cameras may be found. These departments usually collect on more than one subject, but in most cases, the items are irreplaceable.

In contrast, a special library collects in a particular field, whether the materials are rare or easy to get. Often there's a mix, but the emphasis is on the subject, not the value of the items. Special libraries may be maintained by hospitals, colleges and universities, and large financial institutions including banks and brokerages.

Special collections or libraries that collect everything possible on a single topic are invaluable to researchers. For example, the military intelligence collection of the George C. Marshall Research Foundation and Library in Lexington, Virginia, not only collects books, pamphlets, technical papers, periodicals, microfilm, and newspaper clippings, but also diaries, children's cryptographic game books, spy fiction, code items from the Civil War, and examples of ancient Aztec, Inca, and Mayan writings. With so much material on the subject housed in one place, a researcher can detect relationships and patterns that are difficult if not impossible to note when the material is scattered. Furthermore, the staffs of such libraries can usually answer detailed questions in their field, too.

Call before visiting a special collection, especially if it's part of a larger organization. It may keep hours different from the main library or institution that houses it.

Newspaper libraries

Many newspaper libraries have reference collections for their staffs to use in verifying facts. Their most valuable asset, however, is their own newspaper, which they usually clip and batch into subject files. Reporters use these files for quick access to previously written articles when updating an old story. Writers find the clipping files extremely useful, too. Unfortunately, an increasing number of newspaper libraries are closing to the public or limiting service because of the high cost.

Many newspapers will refer you to local libraries, which subscribe to their newspaper and often index it, too. The information from the newspaper is therefore still available, though not in a unique clipping-file arrangement. (See chapter 10 for more information on newspaper libraries.)

HOW TO FIND LIBRARIES AND SUBJECT COLLECTIONS

The following directories identify libraries of every type in the United States and Canada, from zoo libraries to museum libraries.

These directories vary, so note their differences. They also overlap to some extent and may even provide different information on the same library. As in most research situations, it helps to check more than one directory.

1. *American Library Directory (ALD)*. Jaques Cattell Press/R. R. Bowker Co. Annual, with supplement.

ALD lists over 30,000 U.S. and Canadian libraries of all kinds: public, academic, company, museum, newspaper, special subject, private, historical society, hospital, church, bank, military, government, law, association, etc. with subject strengths, collection size, etc. It is arranged alphabetically by state.

Since *ALD* has no subject index, it is best used to get information on a library whose name you already know or to identify libraries in a particular city.

2. *Directory of Special Libraries and Information Centers (DSLIC)*. 5 vols. Gale Research Co. Issued every two years with supplements.

DSLIC lists special collections and departments of libraries rather than libraries as a whole, but covers the same scope of libraries as *ALD*, giving similar information. It is arranged alphabetically by library regardless of its geographic location. A separate geographical volume offers the latter arrangement. The set includes a subject index.

3. *Research Centers Directory (RCD)*. Gale Research Co. Published every three to four years with supplements. Also available in microform.

RCD lists science and humanities research centers that respond to public inquiries. These include herbariums, observatories, and laboratories that are part of universities, government agencies, companies, foundations, associations, and other organizations.

Arranged in chapters of broad subject categories, *RCD* is indexed by subject, location, and research-center name.

4. *Directory of Historical Societies and Agencies in the United States and Canada*. American Association for State and Local History. Issued every three years.

This directory names historical and genealogical societies in the United States and Canada. (Many historical societies are listed in the first two directories above.) It is arranged geographically.

5. *Subject Collections (SC)* by Lee Ash. R. R. Bowker Co. Published approximately every five to seven years.

SC identifies the subject collections of more than 7,000 academic, public, museum, and historical society libraries nationwide. It is arranged alphabetically by subject.

6. *Writers Resource Guide (WRG)* edited by Bernadine Clark. Writer's Digest Books. Updated approximately every three years.

WRG lists some 1,600 foundations, associations, government agencies, companies, museums, historical societies, and special collections, with information on the specific services they provide, how to contact them, and other research tips.

It is arranged in thirty subject categories (chapters) and indexed by subject and organization name.

WHO ELSE GIVES INFORMATION?

The list below is a sampling. Approach most of these sources through their public relations offices (sometimes called community relations or public affairs offices).

Local branches of federal and state governmental agencies

Branch offices of such agencies as the Internal Revenue Service provide varied information and service, including free telephone tips, informational brochures and pamphlets, and seminars.

State, federal, and county agricultural agencies disseminate information about crops and pests in their areas and homemakers' tips, among other things. National and state legislators with local offices dispense information and documents on state and federal issues.

Hospitals and clinics

Many health care centers offer innovative programs and conduct unique research. They may allow you to visit their kidney transplant center, for example, or interview physicians and patients with interesting stories to tell.

Consulates or embassies

Foreign consular offices provide varied information about their countries, from the courses taught in their universities to travel tips. Commercial liaisons handle business information and may distribute such things as lists of product wholesalers and import restrictions.

Trade, professional and other associations

Most organizations, whether they're groups of thimble collectors, amputees, UFO-watchers, or teachers of the gifted, issue brochures, newsletters, or magazines about their common interest. Check *Encyclopedia of Associations* and *Writer's Resource Guide* to identify such groups.

Chambers of commerce

There are more than 7,000 chambers of commerce in the United States, and many foreign chambers of commerce maintain offices here—for example, the Netherlands Chamber of Commerce in New York City. A chamber's task is to attract income and investment to its area through business and tourism. It provides statistics, photographs, economic reports, and surveys concerning taxation, local products, hotel rates, convention facilities, import and export tariffs, etc. Public or academic libraries in its area also may own copies of its reports.

As you can see, the list of information sources is unlimited and extends as far as your imagination.

2
QUICK-AND-DIRTY RESEARCH

In more than a decade of helping people find answers, I've found that most research falls into two categories: quick-answer research and in-depth research.

Questions that call for a pat or quick answer—a short why or how-to response, a fact, statistic, address, or quantity—may take a few minutes to an hour to research. Sample questions are, "What's the address of *The New York Times*?" "When and where did the *Titanic* sink?" "What kind of measure is a kilo-pond?" "What are the rules of rugby?"

Questions that require in-depth probing result in a history, analysis, interpretation, or full-length book; "How can I trace my roots to Charlemagne?" "What kind of life resides in the ocean?" "What is dyslexia and how is it treated?" In-depth research usually takes several steps, various resources, and many hours, days, or weeks of work.

QUICK-ANSWER RESEARCH

Three quick-and-dirty approaches work well for answering many questions fast, and they don't require great skill. They work best in the reference sections of *large* libraries.

STEP 1. Use reference books: directories, almanacs, encyclopedias, and dictionaries

Reference books are arranged in formats that encourage consultation rather than reading. That's why they comprise the major portion of a library's reference section. (See chapter 5 for specific tips on using reference books.)

To determine who sells books in Japanese, you'd check the *American Book Trade Directory*; to find the meaning of *copacetic*, you'd use a dictionary of slang. You'd check the *College Blue Book*, among others, to identify colleges that teach veterinary medicine. To find the winners of events in the 1936 Olympics, you'd try an almanac. The guides on page 10 will help you identify the right reference book to use.

STEP 2. The subject approach

You're stuck. You don't know what to do. Another approach you can take is to zero in on the subject of your search. That means going to the reference shelf where books on the subject are grouped and trying different ones.

For example, someone once asked me to describe the duties of a "best boy" and a "key grip," jobs usually listed in movie credits. I was duly cautioned that the terms weren't listed in the "regular" dictionary.

I went to the film reference shelf and browsed. I found the terms described in a specialized dictionary of motion picture terms. (The terms also appear in dictionaries of occupations in the business section.)

STEP 3. Think in categories

Another way to approach finding a quick answer is to categorize. Once you become familiar with general reference books, you'll do this automatically.

For example, to find a manufacturer of doorknobs, I think "manufacturer" and try a directory of manufacturers such as *Thomas Register of American Manufacturers*.

For a list of past Nobel prize winners, I think of directories of prize winners such as *Winners*. And since award winners constitute a "list," I'd try *The Book of Lists* or an almanac that includes many lists.

As you can see, categorizing can lead you to a reference book, sometimes two or three.

THE TWO-OR-MORE-STEP APPROACH

Sometimes the path to an answer is not straightforward. It may require devious or creative thinking on your part to find it. A friend once asked me why he couldn't locate a particular magazine he knew existed. It contained ads to help American men find Asian wives and was published by a former American GI and his Filipino wife.

Since it sounded like a newsworthy story, I suggested he try *National Newspaper Index*, a microfilm index that jointly indexes five of the country's major newspapers for the past three years. He found an article on the front page of the *Wall Street Journal* that gave the couple's home base, among other things. (My friend didn't find the magazine in directories of magazines because the publication was considered a catalog, according to the *WSJ*.)

Categorizing doesn't always work. You might be categorizing differently from other resources, as the above example illustrates.

GUIDES TO REFERENCE BOOKS

The guides listed in the next paragraph will help you find useful reference books for your quick-answer question. These guides are arranged alphabetically by subject: ASTRONOMERS, ATHLETIC FIELDS, ATOMIC WEIGHTS, AUTOMOBILE MANUFACTURERS, AWARDS, BALLETS, BOARDING SCHOOLS, CAROLS, CONGRESSIONAL DISTRICTS, FLAGS, etc. Therefore, if you're looking for a directory that lists product brand names, you'd check the term BRAND NAMES in one of the guides. One source you'll find listed is the *Trade Names Dictionary*.

No guide mentions every possible source, but these books are excellent places to begin a search. Even if the library doesn't own a book they recommend, you can borrow a previous year's edition through interlibrary loan or ask the librarian to suggest another title that gives the same information.

1. *Concise Guide to Library Research*, by Grant W. Morse. 2d ed. Fleet Academic Editions. 1975.

2. *How to Do Library Research*, by Robert Downs and Clara Keller. University of Illinois Press. 1975.

3. *Where to Find What: A Handbook to Reference Service*, by James M. Hillard. Scarecrow Press. 1975. Rev. ed. 1984.

4. *Where to Find More: A Handbook to Reference Service*, by James M. Hillard. Scarecrow Press. 1977.

5. *Finding the Source*, by Benjamin Shearer and Barbara Smith Shearer. Greenwood Press. 1981.

IN-DEPTH RESEARCH

Eventually, you'll need more than a simple address or encyclopedia article. You may have to do long-term research that incorporates many sources, not just one or two.

Regardless of the subject, research follows a pattern. The chapters in this book are part of that pattern. In most instances, you'll check one or more of the following resources:

1. Periodical articles

2. Books

3. Encyclopedias

4. Reference books (directories, almanacs, etc.)

5. Government documents

6. Original research (private papers, public records, etc.)

7. Experts and organizations

It's not necessary to follow the sequence above. This is merely a guide to help you approach each research problem consistently. As you do more research, you'll become more skilled in following your own instincts. The sample searches in chapter 19 will show you how the in-depth approach works.

The important thing I've learned about research is that it's easier than it appears. With a plan and a good library, you'll uncover more information than you believed possible—and with far less effort.

3
SIDESTEPPING THE RULES

"**I**'ve tried *everything!*" Does this cry sound familiar?

There are many reasons why you can't always find answers or information the first time you look. But if you know the major research obstacles that await you, you can sidestep them and make your work easier.

FINDING BOOKS BY SUBJECT

It helps to know, at least broadly, the subject classification systems most libraries use to arrange books on their shelves: the Library of Congress (LC) system and the Dewey Decimal (DD) system.

For example, a journal called *Gymnasium* sounds like a sports magazine but its LC classification (L) indicates that it's an education title. (Sports falls in the G's). What's the topic of a magazine called *Hispanic Review*? Its LC classification, P, indicates that it's a literary magazine. Knowing at least the broad subject of a book or magazine can help you avoid wasting time going in the wrong direction.

The Dewey Decimal System

The DD system is straightforward and uncomplicated. With its limitations on expansion, it is used primarily by small libraries.

The broad DD system looks like this:

000 General works	500 Natural science
100 Philosophy	600 Useful arts
200 Religion	700 Fine arts
300 Social science	800 Literature
400 Language	900 History, biography

The Library of Congress System

The LC subject classification is used by large libraries. The complete version occupies several volumes. A broad version looks like this:

A	General works
B	Philosophy, psychology, religion
C	Auxiliary sciences of history (archaeology, genealogy, etc.)
D	History: general and Old World

E, F	History: America
G	Geography, anthropology, recreation
H	Social science
K	Law
L	Education
M	Music and books on music
N	Fine arts
P	Language and literature
Q	Science
R	Medicine
S	Agriculture
T	Technology
U	Military science
V	Naval science
Z	Bibliography, library science

SPELLING AND TERMINOLOGY TRAPS

Catalogs

Library catalogs can prevent you from finding what you want in many ways. Some of their traps appear as spelling variations (medieval, mediaeval; Coffman, Kaufman), archaic terms (European War instead of World War I), or misfilings.

Computer catalogs will resolve most of the problems inherent in fixed card files, but you'll continue to use more than catalogs in your work. You'll rely on reference books that follow the same filing and terminology rules as card catalogs, and these will remain with us for a long time.

Unusually worded subjects

Another problem you'll encounter in research is awkwardly worded subjects. Not every topic is expressed as simply as NARCOTICS or SCULPTURE. Books on the Civil War, for example, appear in many printed sources under UNITED STATES—HISTORY—CIVIL WAR, 1861-65. Books on the movies file under MOTION PICTURES.

Terms may be phrased ambiguously—for example, STUDENTS/YOUTH. Geographical areas may overlap—for example, ENGLAND/GREAT BRITAIN.

Some subjects are buried within other subjects (collecting almanacs within books on paper collectibles). Or you simply may be searching the incorrect term (FREEDOM OF RELIGION instead of RELIGIOUS LIBERTY).

Before you look for books on a subject, you must determine the term or even the arrangement of words they're filed under. It's not always easy, but trial and error and perseverance work best. Keep alert for cross-references and other clues to the proper term.

One good clue may be found on the copyright page of another book on the same subject. It may include a copy of that book's catalog card information (called Library of Congress Cataloging in Publication Data). However, the information is only found in books of publishers participating in the program, which started in 1971. If there is an entry, it will conclude with a list of terms that identify the precise subjects of the book and also tell how the subject headings are worded. (See item 10 in figure 3.1.)

Figure 3.1. Sample Catalog Card

BF[1]	Gould, Stephen Jay.[2]
431	Mismeasure of man[3] / by Stephen Jay
G68	Gould. — 1st ed.[4] — New York:[5]
1981	Norton,[6] c1981.[7]
	352 p. :ill. ; 22 cm.[8]
	Bibliography: p. 337-344.
	Includes index.[9]
	1. Intelligence tests—History. 2. Ability—testing—History.
	3. Personality tests—History. 4. Craniometry—History.[10]
	I. Title.[11]

Key:
- 1—Call number
- 2—Author, editor, or compiler
- 3—Title
- 4—Edition
- 5—Place of publication
- 6—Publisher
- 7—Copyright date
- 8—Collation (number of pages, illustrations, charts, tables, etc., width of the book in centimeters. The physical description helps distinguish among editions.)
- 9—Notes
- 10—Subject tracings (those with Arabic numbers. They're selected by the book's cataloger from a standard list).
- 11—Added entries (those with Roman numbers. These most often record a co-author's name and title.)

Filing rules

The alphabet is not as simple as it seems. *B* does not necessarily follow *A*. Two different filing systems, resulting in different arrangements of terms, coexist in printed catalogs, indexes, and reference books. These filing systems are called *word-by-word* and *letter-by-letter*. The word-by-word filing arrangement observes spaces between words and punctuation marks. The letter-by-letter system ignores them, taking each letter in the order in which it appears.

In table 3.1, note how the arrangements of book titles turn out differently when the two filing systems are used.

Table 3.1. Two Ways of Alphabetizing

WORD-BY-WORD

(Note that spaces *are* considered in this filing arrangement.)
Robert Schumann, his life and work
Roberto Matta, paintings and drawings, 1971-79
Robert's Rules of Order
Robertson's Colony in Texas

LETTER-BY-LETTER

(Note that spaces *are not* considered in this filing arrangement.)
Roberto Matta, paintings and drawings, 1971-79
Robert Schumann, his life and work
Robertson's Colony in Texas
Robert's Rules of Order

OTHER OBSTACLES

Magazines at the bindery

Another hurdle to overcome occurs when recent magazines go to the bindery. Having loose issues bound together like a book is convenient—except when they're out just when you need one of them.

If you must have an article, request it on interlibrary loan (see chapter 4), even if it winds up arriving simultaneously with or after the return of the bindery issue. Also check to see if your library has a duplicate subscription on microfilm. Many libraries are buying magazines in this format.

Oversized books

Libraries constantly battle the problem of space. They often shelve very large books (also called oversized or folio books) in a section apart from others on the same subject to use space more economically. This arrangement may cause you to miss an important title. When you're shelf browsing, remember to check the oversized or folio section for other books on your topic. You may find an untapped bonanza.

Closed stacks

Many libraries have closed their book stacks because public access resulted in a high book-loss rate and disorganized shelves. Closed stacks mean that someone else must get your books for you. This procedure takes time, and you can't browse the shelves in hopes of making lucky finds.

If you're working on an in-depth project, ask the head librarian for a stack pass. Exceptions are often made for serious researchers.

One way to partly circumvent closed stacks is to ask permission to use the library's inventory record, the shelf list. This special file is usually kept in an employee work area. Entries are arranged in the same order as the books appear on the shelf—that is, by their call number. The shelf list identifies the books that should be on the shelf, whether or not they're actually there.

Separating books on the same subject

It's not unusual to see books on one subject shelved in two different places, making shelf browsing only partially successful.

For example, many books on summer employment are filed in the HD's, the Library of Congress's classification for labor and employment. Summer employment guides for students, however, are shelved in the LC's (education). Though researchers seldom split hairs so finely, the situation lives on. Rely on the library's catalog to pull together publications that are shelved apart.

Library hours and parking

Always call before you visit a library. Public libraries may change their hours in the summer or close on holidays that are different from those of other organizations. Museum and historical society libraries may be closed on Mondays.

Academic libraries change hours during semester breaks and vacations. Some close early on Fridays, extend hours during finals, or remain open to midnight on weekends. Their branches may keep hours different from the main library's.

If you call first, you'll not only avoid a problem with hours, but the librarian may be able to refer you to more relevant material elsewhere and possibly save you a useless trip.

Finally, parking is a serious problem at some libraries; calling first gives you the chance to ask about visitor passes, fees, or special hours when parking may be free.

Careful planning to reduce frustration will smooth your research path.

4
COMPUTER-AGE SERVICES

The library of the future is here, thanks to technology. Slow service has been streamlined; new services are available. The chances of getting the research material you need are better than ever.

COMPUTER AND MICROFILM CATALOGS

Computer and microfilm catalogs are replacing card catalogs with a faster and more efficient way to find the materials you need. Now you can look for books on a TV screen rather than in a file. You no longer need to struggle with fixed subject headings because you can search for books by keyword.

Another bonus of computerized catalogs is that they can cover the holdings of many libraries within a county or state; so several libraries within a region may share a single catalog. Local interlibrary lending then becomes a routine process, with book delivery by van among the regional libraries. Thus more books are readily available to you.

Computer catalogs are more flexible than microfilm catalogs, though both have benefits. The microfilm catalog is actually a reproduction of the card catalog, and you use it in much the same way. You must wind through the reel until you reach the section of the alphabet you need. With a computer catalog, you need only key in the title of your book or your subject keywords, and a list of books appears on the screen. Both new kinds of catalog offer more information than a card catalog, however, and they're easier to use.

INTERLIBRARY LOAN (ILL)

Things have changed with this service that allows libraries to borrow books and articles from other libraries on your behalf.

Though many libraries still impose some restrictions (most libraries won't lend genealogies, current reference books, the latest fiction and nonfiction releases, fragile and valuable books, and magazines), there are many ways around such limitations. And the service is now faster, thanks to computers.

How does ILL work?

All you need to do to use ILL is fill out a request at your nearest public library—a neighborhood or a main branch. You needn't know which library in the country owns the material you want. Some three thousand public and academic libraries participate in a joint computer-cataloging system called OCLC (On-line Computer Library Center, Inc.), which allows libraries to tap into each other's holdings.

If a book is unique in some way—issued in a small edition, or regional, for example—it helps to know who owns it. Until libraries have added ALL their holdings into these computers, some books will be harder to find than others. Normally, however, you needn't provide the name of the library that owns the item you want.

The time it takes to receive books on interlibrary loan has shortened considerably. Still, you should find out your library's normal turnaround time and if your book doesn't arrive within that time, follow up on the request.

Also ask about possible fees. The service is usually free, but occasionally a lending library may charge for photocopying articles or for book or microfilm insurance.

New materials to borrow through Interlibrary Loan

Because of the greater number of materials now on microfilm and in reprint, materials previously off limits for ILL are now available. For example, the nine-page pamphlet entitled *A Brief and True Narrative of Some Remarkable Passages Relating to Sundry Persons Afflicted by Witchcraft at Salem Village* (Boston, 1692) is in microform, and Henry Fielding's *An Enquiry into the Causes of the Late Increase of Robbers, Etc.*, a 128-page book published in 1751, can be read in a 1975 reprint. In the past, old and fragile items were not only unavailable for loan, but many couldn't even be used if you traveled to the library that owned them. Reprinting and microfilming have made the difference.

RESERVING A BOOK

A frequent complaint of researchers is that books are off the library shelf when they need them most. If this happens to you, try the new streamlined ILL or the reserve or notify system.

Through the reserve system, your public library contacts you when the previous borrower returns a book. If your library doesn't presently offer the service and computers are appearing on the scene, ask about new services that may result from their use. The reserve system may be one of them.

If you own a fee card at an academic library, check the privileges that come with the card. They're usually more limited to the public than they are for the school's students and faculty.

BORROWING REFERENCE BOOKS

Most people think it can't be done. But there are ways.

Libraries that offer a reference service—that is, a service to answer questions for people who come in or call—need a certain basic collection of reference books—directories, encyclopedias, etc.—nearby to provide the answers.

Though librarians try to pick reference books that provide quick answers and that library users probably will not need for extended periods, not all reference books fall into pat categories. A travel writer might want to spend an hour gathering the names of large newspapers that carry a travel section from *Working Press of the Nation*, for example.

Since librarians need quick access to their reference books, you can't check them out. If you ask, however, you may discover that some libraries lend them overnight. The library may also own duplicate copies. Or it may let you borrow last year's edition. (Be sure to watch for out-of-date information in such books. Selected items can be updated quickly with the library's current edition).

Also note that some libraries keep an extra set of encyclopedias and allow borrowers to take individual volumes home. Since encyclopedias don't change much from one edition to another, you may also be able to borrow back sets libraries keep in the stacks.

REFERENCE SERVICES

Research center networks

When a librarian can't answer your question, she or he may pass it on to a research center that serves several libraries in your area.

Most research centers are headquartered in a large public library with auxiliary staff stationed in neighboring public and/or academic libraries. They exist to handle the toughest or most time-consuming questions.

Librarians at research centers operate differently from librarians stationed at reference desks in their home libraries. The research center librarian is more mobile and can check an entire library, not just the reference section. He or she can also make long-distance calls and use electronic databases, services not normally offered at general reference desks.

If you want to pursue your question beyond the resources of a given department, ask the librarian for further suggestions.

Telephone reference service

Most large public libraries provide reference service by phone. There are limits on a librarian's time, so long or complicated questions can't always be tackled.

Try local academic libraries, too. Many handle telephone reference questions from any caller without asking their affiliation or identification.

No matter which library you call, be prepared for busy signals. You may have more luck during off-hours such as dinnertime—although this may also be the time substitutes are on duty.

Also, if you're sure the library is open when you're calling (even though the phone has rung fifteen times), hang on. The librarian may be busy with someone else and can't get to the phone promptly.

Computerized reference service

Many reference books and periodical indexes are available on computer, and many libraries are subscribing to them. By computer, then, the librarian can "look up" the answer to a question or scan periodical indexes. (See chapter 7 for an in-depth explanation of a computer search through periodical indexes.)

At this time, computerized information services offered through libraries are the same as those offered in the private sector by free-lance searchers. The systems are not yet user-friendly and require the intervention of a trained searcher; and they are expensive. Therefore, libraries usually pass on to you the cost of subscribing to and using database services.

Home computer users with modem attachments have access to a scaled-down and easy-to-use version of these services through Knowledge Index (Dialog Services, Palo Alto, California). Though a search through its subdivision, Magazine Index (discussed in chapter 7) may cost four or five dollars, the price may be reasonable compared to the cost of the time, gasoline, and parking fees involved in a trip to the library.

Several directories list a variety of computer databases that are available and the information they provide. One such is *Omni's On-line Database and Directory* by Mike Edelhart and Owen Davies (Macmillan, 1983).

Keep tabs on new and changing library services. They'll save you a great deal of time and effort.

5
SOME RESEARCH TIPS

Sharpen your pencil. You'll soon begin opening books, selecting material, and taking notes. As you do, however, you'll want to be efficient (efficiency = time saved).

We'll first look at books themselves. Many will challenge you to find information in them. Your research habits can slow you down, too. To help you make the best use of your time, we'll quickly review some valuable tips from experienced researchers.

ABOUT BOOKS
Don't judge a book by its cover (or title)

Sometimes the best part of a book is its title. Conversely, reference books often have dull titles, yet they include huge amounts of information—far more than their titles or tables of contents suggest. For example, the *Encyclopedia of Associations* includes listings for chambers of commerce and book clubs. The *Ayer Directory of Publications* lists nationwide newspapers; the *ZIP Code Directory* includes street addresses for hospitals, hotels, and military bases in major cities.

If a reference book is on the broad subject you're searching, check it. It probably contains extras.

Use more than one book on the same subject

Books written on the same subject are often as different from one another as their authors. One book on dinosaurs may be short and sketchy, another may be comprehensive and long. Some books are readable, others are not. One book may emphasize one aspect of a topic, another book may focus differently. Compare two dictionaries of slang, for example, and you'll find that each includes some terms the other does not. The question you're researching may not be impossible to answer at all. You may simply be using the wrong book.

Routinely check several books on the same subject. The data you need may be in one book you try but not in another.

Know how a reference book is arranged

The previous chapter demonstrated how alphabetical order varies with different filing systems. The way reference books are arranged can similarly deter you. Many directories must be used, for instance, from back to front. The publication titles mentioned in *Directory of Directories* and *Writer's Market* are arranged in subject chapters, then alphabetically within those chapters. If you look for a directory or magazine in strict alphabetical order in those books, you won't find it. You must use the index first.

Some telephone books interfile residents of all communities covered; others separate them into different sections.

If you don't notice unexpected arrangements when you open a reference book, you may miss what you're after.

Be wary of book indexes

Book indexes also vary greatly. Some are skimpy, some are detailed; some separate personal names from subjects (thus creating two indexes), while others integrate all terms into one alphabet. Some books omit an index entirely. As a result, information may be in a book but not reflected in the index. This is one reason I often flip through a book and check the table of contents before abandoning it.

In looking for information, an index is essential. Imagine trying to find a product in a Sears catalog without one, especially when you're in a hurry. Remember this when you create the index to your own book. You'll also want to avoid the weaknesses you observe in other book indexes.

ABOUT THE RESEARCH PROCESS

There's more to research than copying information from books and articles. The way you approach your research results in time lost or saved. Here are some tips to consider.

Do you really need that particular book?

People often ask me to help them relocate a particular book when they're really looking for something on the subject.

Don't sabotage yourself by insisting that you must find *The Allergy Self-Help Book* when it's really information on allergies that you want. *Subject Guide to Books in Print* will identify many books on almost any subject.

Follow leads and hunches

Not all research follows a straight path leading to The Answer. Perhaps you'll use some creative thinking or follow clues to find it.

A person once asked me to identify "Glubb Pasha," a term she kept encountering in her readings on India. I found nothing on it in the *Cyclopaedia of India* under Pasha, so I checked the term in the *Encyclopedia Americana*. It said that Pasha was a title conferred on senior civil and military officials of the Ottoman Empire and Arab lands and that the British general who commanded the Arab Legion in Jordan until 1956 was called the Glubb Pasha.

As you can see, this didn't answer the question. Now what? Since there was no entry under Glubb, I took a chance and checked under Arab Legion. There I found complete information on Sir John Bagot Glubb.

Select the right amount of information—then stop

The size and depth of any project will dictate the number of books and articles you research. That's not to say you'll find the precise amount of information you need. Sometimes you'll find too much, and other times, not enough.

If you find too much information, you'll have to sort through it. For example, countless words have been written on American-Soviet relations. In getting background for your article on the topic, you'll discover hundreds of articles listed in periodical indexes. The task of choosing among them will be awesome. How do you do it?

Information becomes repetitive, so you needn't worry about reading *every* book or article on a subject. In the beginning, you must read most of what you find. Soon you'll start skimming, because much of the information has become familiar. On the other hand, if the data run out, you'll automatically stop.

If you find little or nothing on a topic you suspect should be covered, recheck your facts. If you've copied something incorrectly—a date or a spelling—it can derail you.

Know how and who to ask for help

How to ask. You've gone as far as you can on your own, and you still don't have what you need. Now what? Consult a librarian or some expert for final help. Do it carefully, however. The way you ask your question can greatly affect the answer.

Follow these steps when asking for information:

1. State your problem.

2. Give all the information you have, however sketchy.

3. Tell why you need the information.

Say you want to know the address of a publisher in Charleston, South Carolina. You might possibly ask a librarian: "Do you have the phone book for Charleston, South Carolina?" If she says no, your search is stalled.

You actually asked the wrong question. You don't really care if the library owns the Charleston phone book. You want the address of a publisher in Charleston, no matter where it's listed.

That's your real question, and you must say so—that is, state your problem. "I want the address of a publisher in South Carolina." That way, the librarian or expert knows exactly what you want and can use every available resource, some you'll know nothing about. He or she will categorize your question and present you with several options, not just a phone book. A directory of publishers or a directory of businesses in South Carolina could have the information, too.

Besides stating your problem, telling why you need the information is often helpful to the librarian. Do you want to reach this publisher because it publishes religious books or because you want to trace a particular editor? Maybe you're just looking for any religious-book publisher, and others will do as well. Each problem can take the librarian to different reference books.

Writer's Market is one place to get the publisher's address. If you're looking for a particular editor, *Literary Market Place* will be a better source because it includes a list of publishing-house personnel. If you're simply interested in religious publishers, you may be directed to a how-to book on writing for the religious-book market that includes an appendix of religious publishers by denomination.

Did you forget anything? Maybe you've heard that this press is a tiny one. Can that information help the librarian? You never know. If the publisher isn't listed in either *Writer's Market* or *Literary Market Place*, your extra clue might send the librarian to still another directory—*International Directory of Little Magazines and Small Presses*.

Another tip is to avoid expressing your problem in broad terms. "Give me all the information you have on religious publishing." Wow. If you ask in person, a librarian will get you to narrow your problem to something manageable, but with a mail request, you'll never get an answer.

Who to ask. Cultivate the friendship of helpful librarians who show an interest in your project. They may offer extra ideas and suggestions that enrich it.

Most of the time, however, you'll use the services of different librarians. As a result, the service you get will vary. Like most human beings, librarians have different work experiences, backgrounds, interests, and styles. The same question may elicit different approaches or responses from different people.

People often give wrong answers, too. Once burned, you'll develop the habit of occasionally asking more than one person the same question—discreetly, of course.

If a librarian is busy when you approach, service may be less effective than normal—one reason why it helps to know how to do research yourself.

It's not always possible for librarians to come up with an answer on the spot. They may find it after you've gone and have no way to contact you—unless you leave your phone number or address.

Finally, don't expect a librarian to do extensive research for you. Many writers pride themselves on getting a librarian to spend an hour or more helping them, but this is not typical.

Do your own research whenever possible

If you must ask for someone's help, be prepared for less information than you'd get yourself. Stand-ins cannot answer specific questions about *your* project. They will not recognize bonus information in books or articles that would excite you beyond words. They simply aren't as effective as you would be regardless of their superior research skills.

ABOUT ORGANIZATION

Organization is a must. Nothing is as dangerous as escalating blood pressure resulting from a lost page or note. The tips that follow will help you keep small problems from becoming major traumas.

Write clearly

If you can't read your own handwriting, your career as a communicator could be jeopardized. Did I mean "delay" or "relay"? Many words fit the same context but provide opposite meanings.

Write on one side of the page

Don't write on two sides of some pages and then go crazy thinking you lost a paper. By writing on one side, you can easily spread out pages and see your work at a glance.

Use large margins and wide spacing between lines

Give yourself enough room to add information and revise without constantly having to retype or rewrite the page to read it.

Copy with care

Don't trust your memory. Write it down. Also, watch your *p*'s and *q*'s—and your *l*'s and *b*'s and 2's and 3's. A wrong letter or number can set you off in the wrong direction for hours.

Copy authors' first *and* middle names. More names are common than you think. Is the George MacRae you're looking for George L. or George S. MacRae? Are George MacRae and George L. (or George S.) the same person?

Watch abbreviations

Did that "pub" stand for publication, publisher, or publishing? You can resolve the problem of unknown endings by adding a suffix or the word's last letter to your abbreviation. Instead of writing "Detroit Pub.," write "Detroit Pubg Co." or "Detroit Pubns."

Many publications use abbreviations freely without a key to interpret them. What does "J. Exp. Soc. Psych." stand for? If you figure it out incorrectly, you'll search incorrectly. Eventually, you'll have to retrace your steps to straighten it out.

You'll often have to spell out words to others when conveying information orally. Imagine what happens when a librarian looks for an author's name you've given her under *f* instead of *s*.

Note the sources you've tried

Even when you've found nothing, note the sources you've tried. It will help you avoid repeating steps when you resume the search some other time or ask a librarian to take over. She may want to know what you've already checked.

Also, note the page number, author, title, and even the call number and library from which you borrowed a book so you can relocate the information if you need it. A particular item might be important proof that your editor wants you to double-check or photocopy.

ABOUT LUCK

There's no question that some answers float out of the air. Your hand touches the very book you need before you've started looking for it; you open a two thousand-page reference book to the very item you need; you hear a news report on the very subject you're researching.

Author Max Gunther defined luck as a type of persistence. In his book *The Luck Factor* (Macmillan, 1977), he concluded that luck is simple mathematics—the more times you try, the better your chance of success.

The same thing happens in research. The more time you spend at research, the more information you'll find. Though I normally approach my own research systematically, I still stumble onto answers through sheer luck. Though it's best to stick to a system, serendipity happens to all researchers. And it will happen to you—especially if you help it along.

6
USING BOOKS IN RESEARCH

How do you begin researching a book or article? The following example shows how one writer gathered material for her Civil War romance novel set in the West.

Jean (not her real name) couldn't recall specifics because her system progressed from one accidental step to another. First, she checked her small-town library for histories of the period. From the bibliographies of those books, she copied the titles of other appealing books. (Unfortunately, this spin-off technique, where one book mentions another and that book mentions something else, is too haphazard. It nets you a growing list of books but not necessarily the books themselves.) Jean also visited used-book stores and checked the bibliographies of books there for more titles to add to her list.

She later found a reference "somewhere in print" to some government-published materials on the Civil War. She sent away to "the government" for information. (She couldn't recall the name of the agency.) They sent her a bibliography.

Someone suggested she contact the Arizona State Historical Society. They sent her, yes, another list of books. She also saw a mention of the University of Nebraska Press "somewhere." They sent her their publications catalog (another list of titles). It luckily showed two reprinted diaries that appeared on her list, and she bought them.

Jean liked the idea of using old diaries and decided that she wanted more. She found one in a secondhand-book store. It wasn't on her list, but since she couldn't find most of the books she wanted, she settled for this one. (At no time had she mentioned trying interlibrary loan or a university library as a way to get the titles she was accumulating.)

What Jean acquired at the end of a three-month random hunt for books was a large collection of titles, a handful of books, and fatigue. She could have completed the entire process of identifying her materials in one day.

The first step would have been to begin a planned search through *Subject Guide to Books in Print* (*SGBIP* is explained in more detail later in this chapter). This tool is more than an in-print guide for booksellers and librarians. It's also a bibliography. It lists countless reprints as well as newly published histories. Even if your library doesn't have many of the books *SGBIP* lists, you can get them through interlibrary loan.

As sample topics, Jean could have checked COSTUME—HISTORY;

COOKERY, and AMERICAN DIARIES.

The next tool to try would be a periodical index. Historical-novel writers will find *Writings on American History* or *America: History and Life* to be invaluable indexes to history magazines. (For a detailed look at researching a novel, see chapter 19.)

There's nothing wrong with the spin-off method or using books that catch your eye *when* these approaches work. Your time is better spent, however, using an organized approach.

YOUR CHOICE OF BOOKS

Approximately 40,000 new books are published in this country every year. That's more than 100 books *per day*.

Most books remain in print for a long time. Newly published books are added to each year's offerings, so the number of in-print books now totals over *half a million* books. Libraries and bookstores, however, carry only a fraction of them.

Since we only see a partial picture of what's available, we often assume that books on certain topics don't exist when, in fact, they do.

HAS MY BOOK ALREADY BEEN DONE?

Let's look at another kind of research for a moment—market research.

Before starting any nonfiction book, you must know the competition, and that's more than the books you've seen in libraries or bookstores. The best way to get a more complete picture is to check *Subject Guide to Books in Print* (*SGBIP*), published by R. R. Bowker Co. This guide is part of the multivolume *Books in Print* set. The two other titles in the set cover authors and titles, and most bookstores and libraries have them.

Before writing my book, I checked *SGBIP* to check my competition. I began my search with the term RESEARCH. I found more than 125 titles, though a close look revealed that most of them dealt with scientific research or writing a research paper. After adding other relevant titles listed under LIBRARY SKILLS; LIBRARIES—HANDBOOK, MANUALS, ETC, and other terms starting with the word *library*, I actually wound up with a list of only about two dozen possible competitors.

After I checked these books individually, I saw that none resembled my proposed book.

In certain projects, it's best to find out what people are working on rather than what they've published. For example, if you're contemplating a new biography of Thomas Jefferson because you have new information on him, *and* your project will take several years to complete, it's best to contact other Jefferson biographers or scholars. They often know if someone else is working on the same thing. Simultaneous projects are an everyday occurrence. However, checking *SGBIP* is usually sufficient.

Publishers automatically check it. When you know your competition, you may decide to abandon your project for the time being or change its slant. By giving your book a fresh look, you'll increase its marketability.

MORE ABOUT *SGBIP*

Let's return to *SGBIP* as a tool to use for research. Since it's accessible even to small-town writers *and* since it lists up to 90 percent more titles than you'll ever see in a library or bookstore, it merits close inspection.

Books on topics from abortion to Zulus

SGBIP will help you answer specific questions by identifying books on the subject. If you want to know the name and lyrics of Scotland's national anthem or ways to get help for a fear of snakes, you'll find appropriate books by checking *SGBIP* under NATIONAL ANTHEMS and PHOBIAS. (Old *SGBIP*'s are useful, too, since many books remain in print for more than a decade.)

Textbooks

Paul Achuff hesitated finishing his novel set in Vietnam because he couldn't afford to travel there. But if we wrote only about things we've experienced or places we've visited, few of us would be able to write at all. Effective detective fiction need not be limited to authors with criminology backgrounds. Experience can't hurt, but lack of first-hand knowledge needn't be a barrier. (Robert Parker who writes the Spenser detective novels is a professor of English literature.)

Let's say you want to write that detective novel. How can you learn the behind-the-scenes emotions that permeate a police station or courtroom, the ruses private investigators use to get off-limits information, or the techniques of talking someone off a skyscraper ledge? Is the only way to do it to follow a police officer for ten weeks taking notes?

Of course not. You can also check *SGBIP* for books—textbooks. Most people take courses or attend school to learn their trade or profession. That includes police officers, doctors, cosmetologists, and bartenders, who use such texts as *Fundamentals of Criminal Behavior and Correctional Systems; Cosmetology: A Professional Text;* and *Beverage Management and Bartending.*

Test *SGBIP* yourself. Look under various subject headings. You won't believe what's available. (Entries below exclude ordering information and spell out publishers' abbreviated names for easier reading.)

FIREARMS—IDENTIFICATION
Wilber, Charles G. *Ballistic Science for the Law Enforcement Officer.*
1977. C.C. Thomas.
INSTRUCTIONS TO JURIES
Calhoun, Marcus B., et al. *Suggested Pattern Jury Instructions: Civil Cases.* V. 1. 1980. Univ. of Georgia Institute of Government.

MISSING PERSONS
　　Eriksen, Ronald G. *How to Find Missing Persons: A Handbook for Investigators*. 1981. Loompanics.
POLICE—HANDBOOKS, MANUALS, ETC.
　　Camp, William J., et al. *Search & Seizure: A Manual for Peace Officers*. 1979. Univ. of Georgia Institute of Government.

SGBIP identifies books that give inside information about almost any topic. It also includes books issued by unfamiliar publishers whose products you may not find in libraries or bookstores. Many books like the texts above may be found in community college or law school libraries and bookstores where the courses are taught. You can also borrow the books via interlibrary loan or purchase them directly from their publishers.

The history of underwear and other things

Everyone, everyplace, everything has a history. What's more, there's probably a book about it. Here are some "histories" from *SGBIP* with the term under which it appeared:

PORCELAIN—HISTORY
　　Atterbury, Paul. *The History of Porcelain*. 1982. Morrow.
ROCKEFELLER INSTITUTE, NEW YORK
　　Corner, George W. *A History of the Rockefeller Institute, 1901-1953*. 1965. Rockefeller.
UNDERWEAR
　　Ewing, Elizabeth. *Underwear: A History*. 1972. Theatre Arts.

In using *SGBIP,* you'll discover that not all histories are listed under the subject followed by the term HISTORY. Be sure to skim the titles under a subject heading to determine whether or not histories on a subject are there.

Century-old books

Classics, such as the works of Homer and Longfellow, are constantly reprinted. Many books long out of print are reprinted and then listed in *SGBIP* as "new" copies currently for sale.

Reprints are useful. They give perspectives of past times that aren't always seen in current books. For example, a book written on the Civil War by someone who was there projects a different mood from that of a book published a century later by someone who digested the material from published sources. Since many old books aren't available through interlibrary loan, having them in reprinted editions gives us access to books we normally could not get.

This sampling of reprints from *SGBIP* will demonstrate the variety of books available and perhaps suggest new projects to you.

POLYNESIA—DESCRIPTION & TRAVEL
　　Lucatt, Edward. *Rovings in the Pacific, from 1837 to 1849*. 2 v. 1979 Repr. of 1851 ed. AMS Press

POOR
  Woods, Robert A. *The Poor in Great Cities*. 1972. Repr. of 1895 ed.
  Humanities.
PRISONS—GREAT BRITAIN
  Howard, John. *Prisons & Lazarettos*, 2 v., incl. *State of Prisons in
  England & Wales*. 4th ed. 1975. Repr. of 1792 ed. Patterson-Smith

It's very handy to own a set of *SGBIP*. New sets sell for over $100, but
for as little as $10, you can get last year's edition from libraries or book-
stores that keep only the current year's copy. Naturally, you won't use an
old copy for current information, but you can see how useful back editions can be, especially if you can't get to a large library often.

How to interpret entries in *Books in Print*

Reference books use many abbreviations and symbols. The sample
entry below explains some of those commonly used in *SGBIP*.

Truman, Ruth.[1] *Underground Manual for Ministers'*

Wives.[2] LC 73-23060.[3] 176 p.[4] 1974.[5] 6.95.[6] (ISBN

0-687-42796-7).[7] Abingdon[8]

1. Author.
2. Title.
3. Library of Congress number (chronological number assigned to a
   book when it's cataloged by the Library of Congress).
4. Number of pages.
5. Date of publication.
6. Price.
7. International Standard Book Number. (The ISBN is a unique
   number assigned to every book and every separate edition of a title. It helps libraries and bookstores order books more precisely.)
8. Publisher. (A publisher's name always appears as the last item in
   the entry. Publishers and their addresses appear in the last volume of *Books in Print—Titles*, and also in *SGBIP*.)

Some abbreviations used in *SGBIP* are easy to figure out. *Pap.*, for example, stands for "paper copy"; *ed.* means "edition"; *vols.* means "volumes"; *illus.* means "illustrations," etc. Check the key for others.

A final note about reading *BIP* entries. Many omit the number of pages in the book listed. Before buying a book mentioned in any resource, ask
a librarian to check other reference sources for you to determine its
length. You might hesitate to spend $9.95 for a book that contains only
seventy-five pages.

BIP is unquestionably valuable, but it only identifies books that are *in
print*. Much research is done from books no longer in print. One way to
find out about such books is to use a subject bibliography.

BOOKS TO FIND BOOKS: BIBLIOGRAPHIES

Bibliography is a word with many shades of meaning. We know it best as a list of publications: books, articles, newspapers, documents, reports, etc. Bibliographies often appear at the end of research papers, books, encyclopedia articles, magazine articles, reports, dissertations, and other works. They indicate which publications the author consulted in preparing this work. Sometimes they suggest readings for further study; they may even occupy a complete book, such as the 352-page *Knute Rockne: A Bio-Bibliography* by Michael Steel (Greenwood Press, 1983). The collection of materials includes references to articles in magazines and newspapers of Rockne's day, including the Notre Dame alumni publications. From the perspective of a researcher considering a new biography of Rockne, this access to a comprehensive collection of previous writings compiled in a single volume is an incomparable time-and-labor-saving device.

Bibliographies can focus on any noteworthy individual or subject, such as *Parent-Child Separation: Psychological Effects of Development; An Annotated Bibliography*. They cover materials in a time period established by the compiler, so you may have to check more than one.

The idea of using a bibliography is to save the time and trouble of culling reading material from many different resources. When you begin your research, watch for a subject bibliography covering your topic. If you find one, you can reduce your search time considerably.

How to find bibliographies

One quick way to identify a bibliography is to check a library catalog or recent or back copies of *SGBIP*.

The following bibliographies are listed in *SGBIP* under their subject headings:

CHRISTIANS IN AFRICA
> *Christianity in Tropical Africa: A Selective, Annotated Bibliography*. 1977. Kraus Int'l.

PSYCHICAL RESEARCH—BIBLIOGRAPHY
> White, Rhea A., & Dale, Laura A. *Parapsychology: Sources of Information*. 1973. Scarecrow.

SPORTS—BIBLIOGRAPHY
> Gilmore, Al-Tony. *The Afro-American in Sport: An Annotated Bibliography*. 1981. Garland Pubns.

As with histories, the subdivision BIBLIOGRAPHY is not consistently used. You'll have to skim book titles listed under the major subject heading to catch all of them.

Large library systems buy subject bibliographies. If a library near you doesn't have the one you need, try borrowing it on interlibrary loan.

BUYING OUT-OF-PRINT BOOKS

You may want to buy instead of borrow some of the out-of-print (OP) books you identify in your research. In that case, contact a local second-hand-book dealer, most of whom offer a search service. Through their contacts with other dealers, they can locate OP books for you.

Once you receive a price quote from a dealer, there's generally no obligation to buy the book. If the price seems too high, try negotiating for a lower price.

One possible way to eliminate the middleman is to consult a specialty dealer who collects books in the subject you want. For example, if you want a specific OP title on historic costume, chances are high that an art-book or theater-book specialist may have it right in stock. It takes just a postcard to find out.

Directories listing specialty book dealers are normally shelved next to each other at the library. Choose the most recent directory. The two below should be available in large libraries:

1. *The Collector's Guide to Antiquarian Bookstores*, comp. by Modoc Press. Macmillan Publishing Co. 1984.

2. *Directory of Specialized American Bookdealers, 1981-82*, by the staff of *American Book Collector*. Arco Publishing. 1981.

Another tip for locating book dealers is to try the Yellow Pages of regional telephone books in the library. Dealers in New England history should be concentrated most heavily in that region; most dealers in books on the Navajos should be in Arizona.

The Manhattan Yellow Pages is also an excellent source to check. It lists numerous secondhand-book dealers and their subject specialties.

BOOKS IN MICROFORM

Many OP books have been microfilmed as parts of large collections. Though these books are theoretically available through interlibrary loan, they actually are not, because many of them are not cataloged. When a library buys a single microform set consisting of hundreds or thousands of books, quick cataloging becomes a problem. As on-line catalogs become more common, however, the individual books in microform sets will soon be cataloged and easier to find.

In the meantime, many of these subject sets still reside in large libraries under their collection names. Though microform books are not as convenient as their print counterparts, the lower cost and space requirements of the format make it possible for libraries to get thousands of old books they would otherwise not buy.

I've listed several microform collections to give you some idea of what's currently available in large libraries.

1. *American Prose Fiction, 1774-1900*. Lost Cause Press (Microfiche). Research Publications (Microfilm).

Contents. These sets contain up to 11,000 titles, the complete work of *every* major and minor American novelist published in America between 1774 and 1900. Many of these works were the "junk" literature of their day, so they were never reviewed and are no longer available in the original. Beyond their use in literary research, the collections are valuable for their historical, religious, social, and philosophical views of the period.

Printed guides. The books filmed for this collection are listed in *American Fiction, 1774-1900*, by Lyle Wright (Huntington Library, 1957-1969, 3 vols).

2. *Early American Imprints* (Series 1 and 2), 1639-1819. Readex Microprint.

Contents. Much of our nation's early literature focused on religious and political topics. This set includes publications on such topics as the Indian/colonial wars and advice on everything from etiquette to chastity and temperance. The set claims to include everything published in America between 1639 and 1819. (Magazines, city directories, and newspapers mentioned in the printed bibliographies above are reproduced in separately filmed collections.)

The collection began filming in the 1950s and numbers more than 100,000 titles.

Printed guides. The microform collection is based on titles in *American Bibliography, 1639-1800* by Charles Evans (American Antiquarian Society, 1949-59; reprinted by Scarecrow Press, 1967; 14 vols.), and *American Bibliography, 1801-19* by Ralph Shaw and Richard Shoemaker (Scarecrow Press, 1958-66; 22 vols.).

3. *Library of American Civilization*. Library Resources, Inc.

Contents. LAC is a collection of 20,000 selected books, book chapters, articles, pamphlets, documents, biographies, fiction, etc. that portray the social, political, and economic growth of America from the eighteenth century to World War II. Much of the collection's contents is duplicated in other microform sets, but its published subject index makes items in the collection easy to identify.

Printed guides. The collection comes with a four-volume printed guide (Library Resources, 1971-72).

You can approach a search most easily through the subject volume of this guide. For example, under DIVORCE, you'll find Felix Adler's *Marriage and Divorce* published in 1905.

Another volume in this set is called the *BiblioGuide Index*. It is useful as a bibliography of the materials included in the collection.

The *BiblioGuide* does not give the publication date or issue number of the magazines in which the articles ran. Refer to the Microbook's author volume for this information.

4. *Western Americana: Frontier History of the Trans-Mississippi West. 1550-1900.* Research Publications.

Contents. This collection features assorted federal and state documents; directories; guidebooks; state and regional histories; memoirs; reminiscences; travel accounts; and primary and secondary histories, many by everyday people who settled and built the West—storekeepers, homemakers, and others. The set covers all subjects: Indian/white relations, urban development, women, conservation, westward expansion, early industry, and the railroads, to name some.

Printed guides. The 7,000 titles in the set were selected for filming from Wright Howe's *U.S.iana 1650-1950: A Selective Bibliography in Which Are Described 11,620 Uncommon and Significant Books Relating to the Continental Portion of the United States.* (Rev. & enl. Bowker, for the Newberry Library. 1962).

Millions of old and new books are at your fingertips in both print form and microform. A few well-planned steps should connect you with any of them.

7
RESEARCHING FROM
MAGAZINES: Using Indexes

The world is flooded with magazines—several times more than the 200 or so that you see on newsstands and in chain stores. This is an advantage for writers. There are a number of ways to use magazines, some you haven't tried before.

Magazines with circulations from under 1,000 to over 6 million are written for different audiences. Some magazines are sold only in specialty shops—railroading maagazines in model train shops, for example. Others are sold by subscription only to teachers, plumbers, lawyers, and others in trades and professions—one reason we don't see *Journal of the American Bar Association, Kidney,* and *Footwear Focus* on newsstands.

More magazines are generated by banks, membership department stores, airlines, and associations. This helps boost the number of magazines published in this country into the tens of thousands.

Though there are many "invisible" magazines, most are potentially useful in research, and many are paying markets for writers.

WHERE CAN I FIND MAGAZINES?

Freelancers find many magazine markets by accident—on a friend's coffee table, in a doctor's office, or at a book sale.

Libraries are sources of varied magazines, too. Small libraries subscribe to perhaps one or two hundred mass-appeal newsstand magazines. Large libraries carry much more—hundreds, even thousands of special-interest, technical, and popular magazines published in this country and abroad.

Finding magazines is just half the battle, however. You must also be able to locate specific articles within them.

THE KEY TO FINDING ARTICLES

The fastest way to find articles in magazines is to use a periodical index. There are *more than 100* from which to choose.

Reader's Guide to Periodical Literature (RG) is the index familiar to most of us. We started using it in high school and continue using it as writers to check the competition for an article idea and to do actual research.

RG is severely limited, however. Of the thousand of magazines in print, it covers less than 200. (*Writer's Market* lists more than 3,500 magazines.) You wouldn't use *RG* to find an article in a specialty medical magazine or for the latest research on the psychological basis of shyness because it doesn't cover the right magazines for those purposes.

With magazines published in all subjects from art to zoology, you must choose the right index covering the right magazines. In most instances, the index you use won't be *RG*.

USING MAGAZINES IN MARKET RESEARCH

Article writers check *RG* to see what has run in other magazines on their subject. There are other indexes you'll want to consider, too. For example, if you want to query *Backpacker Magazine*, you'd check an index called *Access*. You might also try *Physical Education Index (PEI)* which covers sports and athletics magazines. Not only does *PEI* cover *Backpacker* (remember, several indexes cover the same magazines simultaneously) but it shows you what other, similar magazines have printed about backpacking.

Use the list of indexes on pages 43-45 to select the indexes useful in market research. The list includes most of those currently in print.

USING ARTICLES IN RESEARCH

Market research is only one reason you'll need articles. You'll also use articles in researching your actual writing assignments. Be aware, however, that articles from newsstand magazines are not valid for all kinds of projects. In one article I wrote giving tips to graduating high school seniors on how to live on their own, I gathered all my information from interviews and newsstand magazines. Had I needed information on the latest cancer treatments for an article intended for a top women's magazine, I would not have researched the topic from the newsstand magazines except for background information.

Top magazine markets require that their articles contain the latest developments, not warmed-over, secondhand news. If I used studies reported in other national women's magazines, the information would probably be too stale to be sold back to the same market. To get inside information on new research and trends, check scholarly and professional magazines that document original research, studies, and surveys conducted and written by specialists.

A final word on magazine articles. You can also use them as self-help in your writing. There may not always be someone handy to ask about syndicating columns, copyright, or agents when you need help. Even if you've read articles on these topics, you might not be able to find them again.

To get information on these topics, follow the steps described above— check indexes for articles in magazines. The following extract shows some of the relevant articles I found through *Magazine Index*.

LITERARY AGENTS
How to get a literary agent. *Writer* v97-June '84-p21 (4)
COPYRIGHT—LAW AND LEGISLATION
Does copyright really protect nonfiction? Occasionally yes, but
mostly no; here's why. *Publishers Weekly*. v224 - Dec 9 '83 - p28 (2)
SYNDICATES (JOURNALISM)
Syndicates: how they work, and how they can work for you
(newspaper syndicates) il *Writer's Digest* v64 - Feb '84 - p31 (3)

The value of a periodical index is that it tells you exactly where to find
an article *on any subject* when you need it.

FINDING INDEXES

The list of indexes in this chapter is not comprehensive, but it covers
most subjects. I've omitted many highly technical indexes such as *Nuclear
Science Abstracts*. Most magazines are covered by more than one index
(*Journal of Urban Studies*, for example, is covered by five indexes), so you'll
find most of the information you need anyway. If you want to check technical indexes, you'll find them in science libraries.

The list of scholarly indexes and abstracts in tables 7.1 and 7.2 covers
about half of those in print. Before checking them, let's look at indexes
closely to see what they can really do.

Choosing the right index

Indexes, like books, cover more subjects than their titles imply. You'll
use some "obvious" indexes for your particular project and some apparently unrelated indexes, too.

The "think in categories" rules applies here. For example, to research
religious music, think "religion" and "music." This will lead you to *Music
Index* and also to *Religion Index*, where the topic is covered as well.

For a project on juvenile delinquency,you can search several indexes,
such as *Education Index*, *Criminology and Penology Abstracts*, *Psychological
Abstracts*, *Social Sciences Index*, and *Index to Legal Periodicals*, depending on
the focus you want to take.

When you must make a decision about the "right" index based on its
title, remember that indexes are broad. *Art Index* covers archaeology, city
planning, antiques, interior design, and film as well as crafts and fine
arts. *Writings on American History (WAH)* covers theater, politics, business,
literature, science—*everything* of interest in past people's lives. Note below the scope of the articles from *WAH*.

IVAN F. DUFF. Medical aspects of submarine warfare: the human factor
as reflected in war patrol reports [1941-45] *Arch. internal med.*,
84:246-60 (Aug. 1949). [*AMA Archives of Internal Medicine*], vol. 84,
pages 246-60.]

ZEVI H. HARRIS. The growth of Jewish education for girls in New
York City [1905-56]. *Jew. educ.*, 29 (1):32-8 (fall) [*Jewish Education*, vol.
29, no. 1, pages 32-38, fall issue.]
CHARLEY McDONALD HEARD. Hollywood gunmen. *Gun digest*,
13:186-94

Guides to indexes

The directories below identify many of the scholarly indexes and abstracts in print. They're both arranged by broad topic (biological sciences,
for example). A list of indexes by title appears in each directory's index.

1. *Abstracts and Indexes in Science and Technology* by Dolores B. Owen
   2d ed. Scarecrow Press. 1985.

2. *Periodical Indexes in the Social Sciences and Humanities: A Subject
   Guide* by Lois Harzfeld. Scarecrow Press. 1978.

Look for the most recent edition of any guide you use, though older
guides mention standard indexes and they are still useful.

BEFORE YOU DIG IN: TIPS ON USING INDEXES

The following tips will help you use indexes effectively.

Abstracts vs. indexes

Abstracts and indexes both locate articles in magazines but abstracts
include a summary of articles they refer to; indexes do not. Indexes are arranged alphabetically by subject. Abstracts print their subject index in the
back or front of a volume and refer you to article abstracts within the publication by a number.

Although abstracts are extremely useful for their article summaries,
their subject indexes are often too broad to be helpful. An article I once
found in *Sage Urban Studies Abstracts* on municipal car-pooling programs
appeared under TRANSPORTATION, not CAR-POOLING. (The latter
heading wasn't even used.) I found the article only by accident.

What periodicals does the index or abstract cover?

Periodicals listed in an index are usually listed in the front or back of a
volume (though not necessarily every volume). For magazines listed by
abbreviations, you can find the full title of the magazine in the key.

Does the index or abstract cover articles alone?

Many indexes and abstracts cover books, chapters in books, conference proceedings, select newspapers like the *Wall Street Journal*, and government documents as well as periodical articles. The coverage is usually
mentioned in the volume's introduction.

Does the index or abstract include an author approach?

If you want to check an article by an author's name, you must first determine if the index you're using is cross-referenced according to author. Choose an article and check its author in the index to find out.

Abstracts do include separate author indexes, usually at the back of a volume.

Look for cumulations

Most indexes come out from four to twelve times a year. After a year, the library usually receives a hardcover volume integrating all the data from the past year's loose volumes and discards the paper issues.

Searching annual indexes is tedious, especially when you must check five or ten volumes at one time. Look for cumulations that include several years of the index filed in one alphabet. They're faster to search than yearly volumes.

Table 7.1 lists indexes that cover popular magazines. Table 7.2 covers scholarly indexes. (Some indexes, such as *Physical Education Index*, include both kinds of magazines and theoretically belong in both tables.)

FINDING THE MAGAZINE OR PERIODICAL ON LIBRARY SHELVES

Once you've identified a periodical through an index, you must know how to look it up in a library catalog. It sounds simple, but often it's not.

Many scholarly periodicals are not listed under the titles on their covers. If the magazine's title names the issuing association or organization, whether it's a bank, a social club, or a university, you must look for the publication under the organization's name. *Journal of the American Bar Association* is filed under *A*, not *J*. This kind of arrangement keeps all the organization's publications together in a list or catalog.

> American Bar Association. *Bulletin*.
> American Bar Association. *Journal*.
> American Bar Association. *Papers*.

In other cases, periodicals are filed as they are worded. *Journal of British Law* is found under *J*.

Periodical Title Abbreviations, compiled by Leland G. Alkire (3d. ed., Gale Research Co., 1981) will help you transcribe periodical title abbreviations you've forgotten to check in an index key.

WHO INDEXES WHAT

Suppose you want to know who indexes a particular magazine—say *Scholastic Update* (formerly *Senior Scholastic*). *Ulrich's International Periodicals Directory* (R. R. Bowker Co., annual) will tell you.

The information appears abbreviated at the bottom of the magazine's entry in *Ulrich's*. *Scholastic Update* is indexed by *Reader's Guide, Abridged Reader's Guide, Abstrax, Index to Children's Magazines, Magazine Index*, and *Popular Magazine Review*.

Ulrich's is not comprehensive. Two other guides are also useful if you keep their date limitations in mind.

1. *Chicorel Index to Abstracting and Indexing Services.* Chicorel Publishing Corp. 2d ed. 1978.
Alphabetizes some 50,000 popular and scholarly magazines followed by a list of the indexes covering each.

2. *Magazines for Libraries* by Bill Katz and Linda Stern Katz. 4th ed. R. R. Bowker Co. 1982.
Describes approximately 6,500 magazines recommended for small and medium sized libraries. Each magazine entry includes the index or indexes that cover it.

Magazines themselves may offer clues as to where they're indexed. Look for the indexing information in the masthead, the section listing the magazine's staff, near the table of contents.

Also check a magazine's December or January issue. Many magazines include an annual index to their articles.

Some magazines also publish a cumulated index covering years or decades of issues in a separate volume or set. *Scientific American* and *National Geographic* are two magazines that do this.

MAGAZINE RESEARCH BY COMPUTER

Thanks to new technology, most of the indexes mentioned in this chapter can be searched by computer.

Databases that store magazine indexes are called bibliographic databases. They give you a bibliographic citation or reference, not the article itself.

Computerized search services are offered by commercial firms and some large libraries for a fee. Corporations are the major users of computerized literature searching, since the cost is high, presently ranging from $10 to more than $300 an hour per database. A single search, however, can average $30 or less, and at times you might want to consider having a computer search.

Let's say you want information from periodicals on learning disabilities among children of migrant workers.

You might start your search by checking *Education Index, Social Sciences Index,* and other pertinent indexes under LEARNING DISABILITIES. There's only one problem. The topic is too broad, and you must scan every article under the term to see which ones specifically tie in learning disabilities with children of migrant workers. The terms CHILDREN and MIGRANT WORKERS present the same problems. They're too general.

This topic is a perfect candidate for a computer search. When you want two or more distinct subjects to cross, the computer will do it in a way that you cannot quickly accomplish with the printed indexes. The computer scans keywords from the articles themselves or their abstracts and finds the articles for you.

Your computer search starts with a presearch appointment. You'll select the indexes you want to search and choose primary and alternate terms from the index's thesaurus that describe your topic. (The computer recognizes only acceptable terms.) This process helps reduce wasted time once you're on-line and time is ticking away at one dollar per minute.

After your presearch interview, the searcher goes on-line, that is, he or she calls the database the search service susbscribes to. The computer connected to the database then begins the search.

The index and time period you designated are selected. Then your preselected words or terms are fed in.

We'll assume that LEARNING DISABILITIES is an acceptable term to search through the index you've selected. The computer may then scan, say, five years of the index and count the number of articles during that period with LEARNING DISABILITIES in the titles or abstracts. Perhaps it will be 273.

The searcher may then key in the word CHILDREN to see how many articles include that word in their titles or abstracts. That would probably elicit many citations, say, 1,500. The term MIGRANT WORKERS (or MI-GRANT WORKER) may elicit 50 citations. The searcher feeds in as many related terms as you have preselected.

When this process is over, the searcher combines the words or terms. For example, the computer may be asked to count articles with LEARN-ING DISABILITIES *and* CHILDREN *and* MIGRANT WORKERS in their titles or abstracts. The result of this search might then be two articles.

Finally, the searcher will print out the two article citations. You must get the articles from the library on your own. Though many articles can be printed out on demand, most often you'll get just the citation. On-demand printing is still quite expensive.

A computer search is thorough and fast. If you're researching a dissertation, book or other long project, a computer search may be worthwhile.

Some academic libraries offer computerized search services, though they may be limited only to their students and faculty. Commercial brokers are appearing in large cities nationwide. Check the Yellow Pages of the phone book under LIBRARY RESEARCH, INFORMATION BROKERS, or similar terms. The library may also be able to recommend commercial brokers.

MAGAZINES ON MICROFILM

Libraries are replacing many of their print runs of magazines with microfilm copies. In time, *all* magazines and newsletters will likely be on microfilm, though large libraries will continue to carry recent copies in the print version. Special photocopy machines can make paper copies from microfilm for about fifteen to twenty-five cents per page.

Micropublishers are also filming many century-old and subject-specialized magazines that are deteriorating and getting lost. Microform's compactness and low cost have made it possible for large libraries to buy old magazines they never owned before.

The collections below derive from print copies and many are indexed.

1. *American Periodicals*, Series 1-3, 1741-1900. University Microfilms International.

Contents. The set reproduces more than 1,000 periodicals. For example, it includes *Ladies' Home Journal* between 1883 and 1907; *The Juvenile Magazine*, for black youth, for 1811-13; and *Merchant's Magazine and Commercial Review*, an early business magazine, for the years 1839-70. They cover events and depict life in the United States from 1741 to 1900.

Printed guide. Poole's Index to Periodical Literature, 1802-1907 indexes many of the magazines in the microform collection. (Several of the magazines included have never before been indexed.)

Also check *American Periodicals, 1741-1900, An Index to the Microfilm Collection*, edited by Jean Hoornstra and Trudy Heath (University Microfilms International). It contains subject, title, and editor indexes to the magazines by title but *not* the articles in them.

2. *Nineteenth Century Reader's Guide, 1890-1899.* University Microfilms International.

Contents. This collection includes fifty-one of the leading magazines of the 1890s. Their articles cover "current" events ranging from Alaska before statehood and the Spanish American War to suffrage, the arts, behavior, and politics of the day.

Printed guide. Nineteenth Century Reader's Guide to Periodical Literature, 1890-1899 (H. W. Wilson Co., 1944).

Some other specialty periodical collections in microform are:

3. *English Literary Periodicals* (200 seventeenth-nineteenth century periodicals)

4. *Missionary Periodicals from the China Mainland* (eleven nineteenth- and twentieth-century magazines)

5. *Periodicals by and about North American Indians on Microfilm, 1923-78*, and annual updates. (90 twentieth century, Eskimo, American and Canadian Indian periodicals)

6. *Periodicals on Women and Women's Rights* (thirteen mid-nineteenth-century and early twentieth-century magazines)

7. *Radical Periodicals in the United States, 1890-1960* (forty-eight periodicals)

8. *Radical Periodicals of Great Britain, 1794-1881* (thirty-three eighteenth- and nineteenth-century magazines)

9. *Two Centuries of British Periodicals* (twenty-two eighteenth-century to early twentieth-century British magazines)

Check large public and academic libraries for a large selection of magazines in print and in microform.

Table 7.1
Popular Periodical Indexes

1. *Access.* John G. Burke, Inc. 1975-date. Issued three times a year.
Covers health, family life, hobbies, jobs, consumer issues, etc. in approximately 150 popular magazines not covered by *RGPL* such as *American West, Family Circle, Playboy, Sports Afield, Writer's Digest, Village Voice,* and over seventy-five city and regional magazines.
Access is divided into an author and a subject section. To search by subject, be sure you're checking that section. Complete article information (author, magazine, issue, date), *except* the article title appears under the author's name in the author section.

2. *Alternative Press Index.* Alternative Press Center, 1969-date. Issued quarterly.
Covers approximately 200 left-of-center magazines such as *Covert Action, Grassroots Fundraising Journal, Gray Panther Network, Medical Self-Care, Mother Jones,* and *Progressive.*

3. *California Periodicals Index.* Gabriel Micrographics, 1978-date. Issued three times a year. (Also comes in a microform set called *California Periodicals on Microfilm.*)
Covers approximately thirty magazines published in California about Californians, their life-styles, and interests. Included are *Los Angeles Magazine, San Francisco, San Diego Magazine, Orange Coast, California Business, California Journal, Pacific Horticulture,* and *Westways.*

4. *Catholic Periodical and Literature Index.* Catholic Library Association. 1930-date. Bimonthly.
Covers Catholic life-styles, family living, faith, education, culture, and other topics of interest to Catholics in approximately 130 magazines such as *America, Living Light, National Catholic Reporter,* and *St. Anthony Messenger.*

5. *Children's Magazine Guide: Subject Index to Children's Literature.* The Guide, Inc. 1948-date. Ten issues a year.

Covers articles on animals, holidays, family, nature, crafts, current events, health, history, etc. in approximately fifty-five children's magazines such as *Boy's Life, Children's Playmate, Cricket, Jack & Jill, Ranger Rick's Nature Magazine,* and *Wee Wisdom.*

6. *Consumer's Index to Product Evaluations and Information Sources.* Pierian Press. 1973-date. Issued quarterly.

Selectively indexes articles that review consumer products and services in approximately 110 magazines such as *Byte, Consumer Reports, Dynamic Years, Family Handyman, High Fidelity, Hot Rod,* and *Sunset.*

7. *Index to How-to-Do-It Information.* Norman Lathrop Enterprises. 1963-date. Annual.

Covers how-to articles in arts and crafts from woodworking and metalwork to needlework and dough art in approximately fifty-five magazines such as *Early American Life, Modern Photography, Popular Science, Woodworker,* and *Workbasket.*

8. *Index to Jewish Periodicals.* Index to Jewish Periodicals. 1963-date. Semiannual.

Covers approximately thirty-five magazines focusing on Jewish interests in education, psychology, religion, current events, culture, etc. such as *Commentary, Hadassah Magazine, Midstream, Moment, Present Tense,* and *Response.*

9. *Index to New England Periodicals.* Atlantic Indexing Co. 1977-date. Issued quarterly.

Covers New England history, politics, life-styles, economics, and residents featured in approximately twenty New England magazines such as *Boston Magazine, Connecticut Magazine, Down East, Maine Times, Vermont Life,* and *Yankee.*

10. *Index to Periodical Articles by and about Blacks.* G. K. Hall Co. 1950-date. Issued annually.

Covers education, medicine, music, theater, civil rights, discrimination, and other topics of interest to Black Americans in approximately twenty-five magazines such as *Black Collegian, Black Enterprise, Ebony, Essence, Jet, Sepia,* and *Urban League Review.*

11. *Magazine Index (MI).* Information Access Corp. 1977-date. Issued monthly. (On microfilm only.)

MI indexes more than 400 magazines including everything covered by *RGPL* and *Access. MI* also indexes new-product evaluations, major editorials, short stories, poems, recipes, and book reviews.

12. *Physical Education Index.* BenOak Publishing Co. 1978-date. Issued quarterly.

Covers fitness and nutrition, injuries, training and coaching, sports psychology, athletes, individual sports, etc. in approximately 175 magazines such as *Backpacker, Black Belt, Golf Digest, Muscular Development, Referee, Ski, Shape,* and many state physical-education journals and newsletters.

Table 7.2
Scholarly Periodical Indexes

1. *Abstracts in Anthropology.* Baywood Publishing Co. 1970-date.

Covers archaeology, ethnology, language, physical anthropology, etc. in approximately 300 periodicals such as *Ecology of Food and Nutrition, Genetics,* and *Journal of Human Stress.*

2. *Abstracts of English Studies.* National Council of Teachers of English. 1958-date.

Covers American and English literature and language, aesthetics, criticism, women in literature, black studies, etc. in approximately 1,500 international periodicals such as *Baker Street Journal, Children's Literature, Victorian Studies,* and *Scottish Literary Journal.*

3. *Abstracts of Folklore Studies (AFS).* American Folklore Society. 1960-75. (Topics in *AFS* are continued by *Humanities Index.*)

Covers mythology, wit and humor, legends, superstition, folk songs and dances, customs, riddles, etc. in approximately 175 periodicals such as *English Dance and Song, Kentucky Romance Quarterly, Hawaiian Journal of History,* and *Skip Jack.*

4. *Air University Library Index to Military Periodicals.* Air University Library, Maxwell Air Force Base. 1949-date.

Covers military training, air accidents, foreign air forces, unconventional warfare, military tactics and strategy, national security, preparedness, etc. in approximately seventy-five international periodicals such as *Asian Defence Journal, Infantry, Sea Power,* and *Soviet Military Review.*

5. *America: History and Life.* Part A, Article Abstracts and Citations. ABC-Clio, Inc. 1964-date.

Covers all aspects of U. S. and Canadian history from the history of theater to the history of education in approximately 2,200 international periodicals such as *Baptist History and Heritage, Diplomatic History, Film and History,* and *Nautical Research Journal.*

6. *Applied Science and Technology Index.* H. W. Wilson Co. 1913-date.

Covers space science, computers, energy, fire technology, food industry, geology, mathematics, mineralogy, metallurgy, oceanography, plas-
tics, transportation, etc. in approximately 180 periodicals such as *Artificial
Intelligence, Food Technology, Laser Focus,* and *Wireless World.*

7. *Art Index.* H. W. Wilson Co. 1929-date.
Covers photography, archaelogy, graphic arts, industrial design, interior design, fine arts, city planning, crafts, architecture, etc. in approximately 140 periodicals such as *Fiberarts, Historic Preservation, Print Review,*
and *Town Planning Review.*

8. *Biography Index.* H. W. Wilson Co. 1946-date.
Assembles biographical articles about politicians, artists, educators,
authors, film stars, scientists, etc.from about 2,000 periodicals covered by
other Wilson indexes. Also indexes biographical books and chapters from
collective biographies.

9. *Biological and Agricultural Index.* H. W. Wilson Co. 1913-date.
Covers animal husbandry, botany, conservation, food science, pesti-
cides, veterinary medicine, zoology, etc. in approximately 200 periodicals
such as *American Nurseryman, Genetical Research, Poultry Science,* and *Pesti-
cide Science.*

10. *Business Index.* Information Access Corp. 1979-date (in microfilm
only).
Duplicates *Business Periodicals Index* (see #11) and covers approximately seventy periodicals more, plus books and *The New York Times* financial
section.

11. *Business Periodicals Index.* H. W. Wilson Co. 1958-date.
Covers accounting, advertising, banking, communications, computers, industrial relations, international business, personnel administration, occupational health and safety, real estate, etc. in approximately 280
periodicals such as *Appraisal Journal, Canadian Banker, Taxes,* and *Trusts and
Estates.*

12. *Child Development Abstracts and Bibliography.* University of Chicago
Press. 1927-date.
Covers learning, perception, psychology, health, the family, educa-
tion, etc. in books and approximately 175 periodicals such as *Brain and
Cognition, Cleft Palate Journal, First Language,* and *Journal of Marriage and the
Family.*

13. *Combined Retrospective Index to Journals in History, 1838-1974.* 11
vols. Carrollton Press. 1977-78.

Covers the history of culture, politics, education, business, etc. in approximately 600 international periodicals such as *Alaska Journal*, *Church History*, *Forest History*, and *Iranian Studies*.

This index is arranged by geographic region, then subdivided by period, broad topic, and keyword-in-title. Unlike other indexes, article entries in the *CRIJ* indexes (also see #14 and #15) are arranged in columns. Periodicals are assigned a number rather than abbreviated. (The key is on the inside front and back covers.)

Another unique feature of the *CRIJ* indexes is that they're complete sets rather than continuously issued.

14. *Combined Retrospective Index to Journals in Political Science, 1886-1974.* 8 vols. Carrollton Press. 1977-78.

Covers political thought from the sixteenth century to date, national minorities, multinational corporations, foreign political ideologies, electoral processes, the military, etc. in approximately 200 periodicals such as *Capitol Studies*, *DAR Magazine*, *Explorations in Economic History*, and *Montana*.

Articles are arranged by broad subject category such as international affairs, then subarranged by keyword.

15. *Combined Retrospective Index to Journals in Sociology, 1895-1974.* 6 vols. Carrollton Press. 1978.

Covers family planning, behavior, health, mass communication, group interactions, etc. in approximately 125 periodicals such as *Human Relations*, *Journal of the History of Ideas*, *Quaker History*, and *Polish American Studies*.

Articles are arranged by broad category, then subarranged by keyword.

16. *Communications Abstracts.* Sage Publications. 1978-date.

Covers advertising, broadcasting, mass communications, journalism, public relations, radio, speech, etc. in approximately 200 periodicals such as *Journal of Consumer Research*, *Journal of Educational Television*, *Journal of Media Law and Practice*, and *Political Communication and Persuasion*.

17. *Criminal Justice Abstracts.* National Council on Crime and Delinquency. 1968-date.

Covers crime prevention, genetics and crime, juvenile offenders, the insanity defense, attitudes on firearms, etc. in approximately 160 international periodicals such as *Adolescence*, *Criminal Justice and Behavior*, *Prison Journal*, and *Victimology*.

18. *Education Index.* H. W. Wilson Co. 1929-date.

Covers preschool to adult education, school administration, audiovisuals, counseling, curriculum materials, teacher education, etc. in approximately 200 periodicals such as *College Training, Day Care and Early Education, Exceptional Children,* and *Western European Education.*

19. *Engineering Index.* Engineering Index, Inc. 1884–date.
Covers structural, mechanical, industrial, chemical, and other kinds of engineering in technical reports, conference proceedings, books, and approximately 1,400 journals such as *Earthquake Engineering & Structural Dynamics, Engineering in Medicine,* and *Industrial Robot.*

20. *Film Literature Index.* Filmdex. 1973–date.
Covers festivals, unreleased films, technical aspects of film, avant-garde films, instructional materials, producers, wages and salaries, women in film, etc. in approximately 135 periodicals such as *China's Screen, Dance Magazine, Film Culture, Village Voice,* and selective indexing from magazines and newspapers such as *Harper's Bazaar, School Arts, Sports Illustrated,* and *Variety.*

21. *General Science Index (GSI).* H. W. Wilson Co. 1978–date.
GSI draws from the publisher's other comprehensive science indexes providing representation in all the sciences—astronomy, biology, botany, chemistry, earth science, genetics, mathematics, medicine, nutrition, oceanography, physics, physiology, zoology, etc. It indexes about ninety representative periodicals such as *Audubon, Evolution, Horticulture, Journal of Heredity, Oceans, Psychology Today, RN Magazine, Science Digest,* and *Weatherwise.*

22. *Hispanic American Periodicals Index.* UCLA Latin American Center Publications. 1974–date.
Covers Hispanic humanities and social sciences—literature and criticism, politics, social conflict, labor unrest, land reform, migration, theater, etc.—in approximately 250 international periodicals such as *The Americas, Estudios Sociales (Chile), Jamaica Journal,* and *Latin American Theatre Review.*

23. *Historical Abstracts.* ABC-Clio, Inc. 1955–date. Part A covers modern history (1450–1914); Part B covers twentieth-century history (1914–date).
Covers all aspects of history in approximately 2,000 international periodicals such as *Arctic, Armed Forces and Society, Balkan Studies,* and *History of Agriculture.*

24. *Human Resources Abstracts.* Sage Publications. 1966–date.
Covers labor disputes, wages and benefits, unemployment, career development, etc. in approximately 325 periodicals such as *Connecticut Gov-*

ernment, Ethnic and Racial Studies, Journal of Psychoactive Drugs, and *Small Town.*

25. *Humanities Index (HI).* H. W. Wilson Co. 1974-date.

HI split off from *Social Sciences and Humanities Index* in 1974. It covers archaeology and classical studies, folklore, history, language, literary and political criticism, performing arts, philosophy, theology, etc. in approximately 210 periodicals such as *Science-Fiction Studies, Theatre Journal, Theology Today,* and *Western Folklore.*

26. *Index Medicus.* National Library of Medicine. 1960-date.

Covers disease control, genetics, psychiatry, dentistry, veterinary medicine, sports physiology, transplants, etc. in approximately 2,600 international periodicals such as *Annals of Allergy, Bulletin of the Menninger Clinic, Currents in Alcoholism, Journal of Antibiotics,* and *Vascular Surgery.*

27. *Index to Legal Periodicals.* H. W. Wilson Co. 1908-date.

Covers military, civilian, and international legal matters from corporation law to family practice in approximately 350 journals such as *Catholic Lawyer, Food Drug Cosmetic Law Journal, Judges Journal,* and *New England Journal on Prison Law.*

28. *Index to United States Government Periodicals.* Infordata International, Inc. 1970-date.

Covers scientific and sociological research performed under government contract, aerospace, law, national defense, the arts, wildlife and conservation, consumerism, and other subjects relating to the work of government agencies in approximately 170 government-published periodicals such as *Endangered Species Technical Bulletin, Fish and Wildlife News, Mine Safety and Health,* and *Recombinant DNA Technical Bulletin.*

29. *International Index to Periodicals (IIP).* H. W. Wilson Co. 1907-74.

IIP comprised *Social Sciences and Humanities Index* from 1965 to 1974. In 1974 it split into *Social Sciences Index and Humanities Index.* See entries #43 and #25 for coverage information.

30. *International Political Science Abstracts.* International Political Science Association. 1951-date.

Covers public opinion, political ideologies, foreign policy, military institutions, etc. in approximately 700 international periodicals such as *Indonesia, Journal of Social Issues, International Problems* (Tel Aviv), and *Politics and Society.*

31. *Language and Language Behavior Abstracts.* Sociological Abstracts, Inc. 1967-date.

Covers audiology, linguistics, educational psychology, phonetics, communication, psychology, etc. in approximately 1,000 international periodicals such as *Cleft Palate Journal, Infant Mental Health Journal, Linguistic Analysis,* and *Russian Language Journal.*

32. *Legal Resource Index.* Information Access Corp.1980-date (in microfilm only).
Covers approximately 600 periodicals and four legal newspapers, overlapping with *Index to Legal Periodicals* (#27).

33. *Music Index.* Information Coordinators, Inc. 1949-date.
Covers classical to rock music, concerts, music abroad, music education, innovative music techniques, composition, music celebrities, etc. in approximately 260 periodicals such as *Latin American Music Review, Opera Digest, Ragtimer,* and *Songwriter's Review.*

34. *Nineteenth Century Reader's Guide to Periodical Literature, 1890-99.* H. W. Wilson Co. 1890-1899.
Covers nineteenth-century current events such as the military, moving pictures, religion, Indians, economics, transportation, farming, family life, travel, foreign relations, etc. in approximately fifty-five, mostly defunct, late-nineteenth-century magazines such as *Harper's Weekly, New England Magazine, Overland,* and *Popular Science Monthly.*

35. *Poole's Index to Periodical Literature, 1802-1907.* Houghton Mifflin. 1887-1908. Reprinted by Peter Smith, 1938.
Covers the same topics as *Nineteenth Century RGPL* in approximately 175 defunct magazines such as *Methodist Review, Popular Astronomy, School Review,* and *Sunday Magazine.*

36. *Psychological Abstracts.* American Psychological Association, Inc. 1927-date.
Covers animal psychology, parapsychology, mental disorders, personality development, marriage and the family, sex roles, etc. in dissertations and approximately 850 international periodicals such as *Applied Animal Ethology, Brain Research, Gerontologist,* and *Perceptual and Motor Skills.*

37. *Public Affairs Information Service (PAIS) Bulletin.* Public Affairs Information Service, Inc. 1915-date.
Covers international relations, economics, current events, commerce, industry, government affairs, law, etc. in approximately 425 periodicals such as *Business Japan, Contemporary Marxism, Police Chief,* and *Review of Income and Wealth.*

38. *Religion Index One.* American Theological Library Association. 1949-date.

Covers church history, the sociology and psychology of religion, liturgical reform, the Bible, women in religion, religious current events, etc. in approximately 200 international periodicals such as *Anglican Theological Review, Pastoral Psychology, Quaker History,* and *Religion in Life.*

39. *Sage Family Studies Abstracts.* Sage Publications. 1979-date.
Covers childhood development, foster care, death, family life, divorce, remarriage, family violence and abuse, etc. in approximately 260 periodicals such as *Journal of Family Issues, Mediation Quarterly, Nursing Times,* and *Youth and Society.*

40. *Sage Public Administration Abstracts.* Sage Publications. 1974-date.
Covers city budgeting and finance, the public interest, policy making, bureaucracy in approximately 275 periodicals such as *Charities USA, Ecology Law Quarterly, Government and Policy,* and *Social Indicators Research.*

41. *Sage Race Relations Abstracts.* Sage Publications. 1975-date.
Covers integration, discrimination, attitudes, education, employment, family relations, health, women, culture, identity, etc. in approximately 130 periodicals such as *Boston Globe Magazine, International Migration Review, Policing London,* and *Radical America.*

42. *Sage Urban Studies Abstracts.* Sage Publications. 1973-date.
Covers employment, economic development, crime, law enforcement, public welfare, taxation, etc. in research reports, dissertations, pamphlets, and approximately 180 periodicals such as *Rural Society, Soviet Sociology, Tokyo Municipal News,* and *Urban Life.*

43. *Social Sciences Index.* H. W. Wilson Co. 1974-date.
SSI split off from *Social Sciences and Humanities Index* in 1974. Covers anthropology, economics, environmental studies, geography, law, criminology, political science, public administration, psychology, sociology, etc. in approximately 260 periodicals such as *Child Welfare, Feminist Studies, Journal of Black Studies,* and *Public Welfare.*

44. *Sociological Abstracts.* Sociological Abstracts, Inc. 1953-date.
Covers the family and socialization, rural and urban sociology, poverty, violence, culture, education, religion, etc. in approximately 1,300 international periodicals such as *Population and Environment, Public Opinion Quarterly, Research on Aging,* and *Small Group Behavior.*

45. *Women Studies Abstracts.* Rush Publishing Co. 1972-date.
Covers women and education, psychology, public affairs, law, mental and physical health, government, family, etc. in books, reports, and approximately 500 periodicals such as *Journal of Homosexuality, Ms,* and *New England Journal of Medicine.*

46. *Writings on American History.* American Historical Association. 1903-date.

Covers the history of culture, business and industry, religion, labor, theater, etc. in approximately 400 history periodicals such as *Chicago History, Cinema Journal,* and *Proceedings of the U. S. Naval Institute.*

8
THE OLD REGULARS: ENCYCLOPEDIAS, ALMANACS, DICTIONARIES, CHRONOLOGIES, AND YEARBOOKS

Encyclopedias are one of the most obvious research tools published. That's why high school teachers prefer that their students use them as little as possible. Writers do more original and creative research than students. Still, encyclopedias play an important role.

Almanacs, chronologies, yearbooks, and special dictionaries are effective resources, too. But we use them far *less* than we should. With directories, these tools are the backbone of a library's reference collection. Each has special talents you may not have tapped.

ENCYCLOPEDIAS

The first known encyclopedias originated in ancient Greece for the purpose of summarizing and transmitting general human knowledge to future generations. The word *encyclopedia*, in fact, comes from the Greek and means "general" (*enkyklios*) "education" (*paideia*).

Though the encyclopedia concept has survived for thousands of years, times have changed. Our knowledge and world have expanded beyond limits imagined by earlier civilizations. Their records can no longer be squeezed into a set of twenty or thirty books. Nor can we entrust most of our research problems to this single resource.

General encyclopedias

Encyclopedias can do great things if we observe their differences, strengths, and weaknesses. They answer specific questions (What languages are spoken in Switzerland?), provide overviews of a broad subject (ENGLAND, CHURCH OF), offer clues and leads when we get stuck, and recommend books and articles to read. Their articles may run less than two paragraphs or reach more than fifty pages.

Though general encyclopedias cover a spectrum of topics—the arts, history, geography, science, etc.—they have distinct personalities. Children's encyclopedias are obviously geared to youngsters, though they're useful for getting a broad look at a complex subject such as nuclear energy. The *World Book* aims at a young adult audience; others, like the *Encyclopedia Americana*, offer more in-depth coverage.

Compare entries in any two apparently similar encyclopedias, and you'll immediately detect differences. Some prefer short articles over long ones. One article may emphasize different points on a topic from another encyclopedia's article.

You might also notice subtle biases or varied viewpoints among encyclopedias. It is easy to spot some viewpoints in the English translation of the *Great Soviet Encyclopedia*. The entry for the Vietnam War is filed under *A*—AMERICAN AGGRESSION IN VIET NAM. The article on the Panama Canal says, in part, "After the Spanish-American War of 1898, the USA intensified its efforts to build a canal with the aim of dominating the western hemisphere."

Like magazines, an encyclopedia's character is shaped by the goals set by the editorial board and the experts or staff writers who contribute to it.

In view of such differences, it pays to check more than one encyclopedia in your information search. An answer may be in one encyclopedia but not in another.

Subject encyclopedias

At times, you'll want to check an encyclopedia devoted to a single topic. Subject encyclopedias may provide a more in-depth or specialized focus than you'll find in a general encyclopedia. Consider the different lengths and focuses of the article on Jesus Christ in the *New Catholic Encyclopedia* (fifty-plus pages) and in *Encyclopedia Americana* (eight pages).

The CANADA article in the *New Groves Dictionary of Music and Musicians* will be different from Canada's entry in the *International Encyclopedia of Higher Education* and *Encyclopedia Judaica*. The first focuses on Canada's music, the second on its colleges and universities, the third on its Jewish population.

Subject encyclopedias also include biographies of people prominent in the field or subject of the encyclopedia—late film director Ozu Yasujiro in *Kodansha Encyclopedia of Japan*, for example. In addition, subject encyclopedias contain more elaborate bibliographies of recommended reading than you'll find in general encyclopedias.

Some subject encyclopedias come in large sets of ten or more volumes; others are one- or two-volume titles such as the one-volume *Encyclopedia of Military History*. These "encyclopedias" include brief, dictionarylike definitions, and they're useful in providing quick answers to questions or more elaborate definitions than dictionaries offer.

Many subject encyclopedias are not recent. Compared with general encyclopedias, they're revised less often. Some have not been updated for decades, yet they remain useful in a historical context—for example, the twelve-volume *Jewish Encyclopedia*, published in 1903-6. Depending on your particular needs, consider the date an encyclopedia was published when you use it.

The select list of subject encyclopedias in Table 8.1 (pages 61-63) covers varied topics. I've omitted encyclopedias that cover specific fields, such as the *Encyclopedia of Library and Information Science,* and those issued in less than ten volumes. They're usually on library shelves next to the larger sets, however, or in their proper subject section, so you'll find them easily.

Old encyclopedias

Most general encyclopedias are revised every one to three years, but these are not major revisions. At best, only about 10 percent of an encyclopedia is actually revised, and updating is concentrated in the sciences and other rapidly changing fields. Major overhauls are done less frequently because of the high expense and the short time between editions.

Entries for static subjects in the arts and humanities—Michelangelo or Charles Dickens, for example—change little through several editions over ten, twenty, or more years. The same article often appears in successive editions. This can work to your advantage, since large libraries keep back copies of encyclopedias for borrowers to check out. Use them with their date limitations in mind.

Very old encyclopedias (fifty years or older) take on a new meaning in research. Many of the subjects covered have changed radically. Instead of becoming useless with age, these encyclopedias reflect the flavor of their time and are useful in historical research.

For example, the article on Racine, Wisconsin, in the *American Cyclopaedia* (New York: Appleton & Co., 2d ed., 1879) mentions the population in 1860 (7,822) and 1875 (13,282), the principal industries (eight wagon factories, eight carriage factories, ten tanneries, five harness and saddle factories, etc.), the condition of the schools and streets, and more.

An old encyclopedia can stir your imagination with fresh ideas. Consider how these articles from the 1879 encyclopedia above might enrich your book in progress: PRISONS AND PRISON DISCIPLINE, PUGILISM, RAILROADS, REFRIGERATION, RICKETS, RIFLE.

How hard is it to find an old set? Many are sitting on the shelves of large (usually academic) libraries waiting for you to check them out, as I did.

ALMANACS

Almanacs and Bibles were the first books to come to this country. There were few newspapers in colonial days, and the settlers used almanacs for information and entertainment. Almanacs did everything from predicting the weather and listing home remedies to printing poetry and stories.

Almanacs today have evolved into reference books that cram bits of information into as many as 1,000 pages.

General almanacs

Despite their low-quality paper, tiny print, and skimpy binding, general almanacs are the best research bargain for the money (about five dollars).

Almanacs compile lists and data from other reference sources: weights, measures, a perpetual calendar, sports and Olympics records, the tallest buildings, longest rivers, names and birthdates of celebrities, lists of U. S. colleges and universities, consumer price indexes, and more.

General almanacs have some differences, but most include the same general information. Even so, you should still check more than one before you abandon a search.

General almanacs in print include:

- *World Almanac.* World Almanac. 1869-date (Issued on microfilm from 1869 to 1974 by Bell & Howell).

- *Information Please.* Simon & Schuster. 1947-date.

- *Reader's Digest Almanac.* Reader's Digest Assoc. 1966-date.

- *Hammond Almanac.* Hammond, Inc. 1979-date.

The *Whitaker Almanack* (1869-date) is the major British almanac. It covers such items as happenings in British TV, opera, dance, current events, and science for the year; overviews of Commonwealth countries; chiefs of Scottish clans; a list of British nobility; and a Parliament summary for the year.

Subject almanacs

Many almanacs are now devoted to single subjects and include a conglomeration of facts, figures, associations, people, and other data concerning that field or topic. The *Army Almanac, A Book of Facts Concerning the United States Army;* the *Astronomical Almanac;* and the *Catholic Almanac* are a small sampling of those in print.

Several almanacs cover geographical regions instead of subjects—*Ohio Almanac* (1967-date), *Texas Almanac* (1857-date), *Canadian Almanac and Directory* (1848-date). These almanacs cover the legal, commercial, statistical, religious, political, social, economic, and educational aspects of life in those areas. They include many addresses—hospitals, associations, colleges, government offices—and lists of names.

Old almanacs

Like encyclopedias, certain information in almanacs seldom changes: biographies of the presidents and their wives; overviews of each presidential administration (up to the date the almanac was issued); histories of world nations; chronology of U. S. history; birth and death dates of historical figures; an overview of U. S. space efforts; prizewinners (academy awards, Pulitzer and Nobel prizes, Olympics), etc.

Use your judgment in deciding when and how to use an old almanac. For example, you won't use a five-year-old almanac for current addresses or recent statistics. Consider, however, the kind of information you can reap from these interesting lists in the 1890 edition of the *World Almanac:*

- Survey of world news of the year

- State officials for the year

- Sporting event records up to 1889

- Postal information and rates

- Party platforms of the year

- Vital statistics such as causes of death in the United States

Not every almanac series currently in print dates back to the nineteenth century. While shelf browsing, you may find other almanacs no longer in print today.

DICTIONARIES

As with other reference sources, dictionaries have varied personalities. You may have to use different ones from time to time.

General dictionaries

Large dictionaries like *Webster's Third New International Dictionary* (Merriam Co., 2,600 pages, about $80) are useful for years, even decades. They often include summaries of grammar and punctuation rules, forms of address, and other bonus information.

General dictionaries aren't all you'll use in your research, however. They don't include every word in the English language.

Phrase books and subject dictionaries

You might need a dictionary of slang to find the slang definition of *cupcake* ("freshman") or a dictionary of euphemisms to define *blow your fuse.* Other useful word and phrase books cover catch phrases (*in [someone's] pocket*); foreign terms used in English (*en flagrant*); obsolete words (*liripoop*); Western words (*hog-tie*); military terms (*Jericho Jane*), underworld slang (*bridge jumper*); and Scotch, British, Canadian, and Australian English.

Subject dictionaries cover terms unique to particular fields, subjects, or professions. The word you want defined might be a special term used by architects (*buoyant foundation*) or public administrators (*pluralization*).

Word and phrase books of the English language are generally shelved next to the general dictionaries. Subject dictionaries are shelved in their respective subject sections. You can also identify them through *Subject*

Guide to Books in Print (SGBIP).
Here's a sampling of subject dictionaries from *SGBIP*:

PRINTING—DICTIONARIES
(More than fifteen such dictionaries define words, phrases, and names
used in printing, such as *Clymer press, fingers, gold leaf,* and *lug.*)
>   Glaister, Geoffrey. *Glaister's Glossary of the Book: Terms Used in
>   Paper-Making, Printing, Bookbinding & Publishing.* 1979. U of Cal. Pr.
>   Savage, William. *Dictionary of the Art of Printing.* 1965. Repr. of 1841
>   ed. Burt Franklin.

PSYCHOLOGY—DICTIONARIES
(More than fifty such dictionaries define words, phrases, and names in psychology, such as *Evil Eye, frontal lobe, Fullerton-Cattell Laws,* and *Ganser's syn-
drome.*)
>   Harriman, Philip L. *Handbook of Psychological Terms.* 1977. Littlefield.
>   Wolman, Benjamin B. *Dictionary of Behavorial Science.* 1979. Van
>   Nostrand Reinhold.

RAILROADS—DICTIONARIES
(There are over five such dictionaries, which define words, phrases, and
names in a railroad context—for example, *boomer, fusee,* and *herder.*)
>   *The New Dictionary of Railroad Working Terminology.* 1980. Railsearch.
>   Forney, Matthias. *The Car Builder's Dictionary.* Repr. of 1879 ed. N. K.
>   Gregg.

Watch for other books that use the word *dictionary* in their titles. Many
are not definition books but varied reference books, such as the *Dictionary
of Battles, Dictionary of Abbreviations, Dictionary of American Proverbs and
Proverbial Phrases, 1820-1880,* and *Dictionary of Altitudes in the United States.*

Old dictionaries. One of the most useful English-language dictionaries to writers is the multivolume *Oxford English Dictionary (OED).* In addition to providing the history of words, it includes archaic word use, obsolete words, and slang expressions. For example, you might want to
know when the word *skulduggery* was first coined so that you don't accidentally use it in your novel before its time.

Each word defined by *OED* is followed by notes and sample sentences
where the word was first seen in print. You'll also get the title, author, and
year of publication of the book in which the sentence ran. One of the definitions under skulduggery, for example, is this:

> 'Malversation of public money.' 1890 N & Q Ser VII X 224. "Some two
> or three years ago, one of the New York papers . . . announced that a
> missionary on the Congo intended to return to America and blow up
> the whole scullduggery; meaning, apparently, to expose the false
> pretences on which money had been collected for the mission."

(The sentence appeared in *Notes & Queries* magazine, series 7, volume 10, page 224.)

CHRONOLOGIES

Chronologies list events in date order. Aside from this simple definition, chronologies are very different from one another.

General chronologies

Besides allowing you to pinpoint the date of a particular event, chronologies let you scan the events—historical, cultural, political—of a year or period of years to get a quick overview of that era without reading extensively in books.

Some general chronologies are more detailed than others and may include much insignificant information.

The Cyclopedia of Classified Dates by Charles E. Little (Funk & Wagnalls, 1900; reprinted by Gale Research Co., 1967), for example, records all manner of events from prehistory to 1900.

It's arranged alphabetically by country (Peru, Portugal, Russia), then by a period of years (varies for each country); finally, it is subarranged by topic (Army-Navy, Art-Science-Nature-Letters, Births-Deaths, Church, Society, State, etc.).

One event mentioned under RUSSIA; ARMY-NAVY is the following:

> 1850 Aug. Seven men in each thousand of the population of Western Russia are enrolled in the army by an imperial decree, adding 180,000 men.

A chronology like *People's Chronology: A Year-by-Year Record of Human Events From Prehistory to the Present*, edited by James Trager (Holt, Rinehart & Winston, 1979) is quite different. It includes many major American happenings and many "firsts" in about thirty categories, such as theater, everyday life, crime, energy, politics, transportation, consumer protection, and literature/publishing. It shows that in 1892, for example, telephone service began between New York and Chicago, the addressograph was invented, the *Toronto Star* began publication, and the Dalton Brothers were killed in a bank robbery in the Oklahoma Territory.

Some of the "firsts" it mentions are these: the first milk bottles were used in Brooklyn in 1879, the first mechanically operated windshield wiper was introduced in 1916 (the first electric windshield wiper came along in 1923), and the first U. S. zoning law was passed in New York City in 1916.

Other chronologies such as *Day by Day: The Fifties*, compiled by Jeffrey Merrit (Facts on File, Inc., 1979) are very detailed, arranging events by the day rather than by year. Events reported cover categories ranging from WORLD AFFAIRS to CULTURE and read like newspaper headlines. For example, under the category U.S. ECONOMY AND ENVIRONMENT, you can read that on August 23, 1953;

Robert Vogeler announces a $500,000 suit against IT&T "for what I went through" during and after his imprisonment in Hungary.

Some chronologies, like the *Almanac of Dates* by Linda Millgate (Harcourt Brace Jovanovich, 1972) are arranged like calendars. They list major events by date of the month, regardless of the year in which the event took place. For example, you'll find that on March 15, Julius Caesar was assassinated in 44 B.C. On that date in 1820, Maine became a state, and on March 15, 1919, the American Legion was organized in Paris.

Other chronologies cover specific topics. Examples include *Chronology of the Ancient World: 10,000 B.C. to A.D. 799* or *Black Chronology from 4,000 B.C. to the Abolition of the Slave Trade.*

Whichever chronology you use, be aware of how it's arranged and the kind and scope of information it covers. Some may be more useful to you than others.

Chronologies in other books

Chronological charts appear as a feature of certain reference books. General almanacs usually include a chronology of major national and international news events of the year and a list of space achievements since the 1950s. The *Dow Jones-Irwin Business and Investment Almanac* includes a chronology of the year's business and finance news. *The Almanac of China's Economy, 1981* includes a chronology of major economic events in China in 1979 and 1980; the *Almanac of American History* is a complete chronology of dates and events in American history.

When you check almanacs and subject reference books, see if they have chronologies within their pages. These listings sometimes turn out to be a large portion of, if not the entire, reference book.

YEARBOOKS

Yearbooks are mini-encyclopedias that report on the latest developments of a particular year.

General yearbooks

General yearbooks are usually arranged alphabetically by subject. If they're arranged by category, they'll include a subject index at the end of the book. Sample subjects they cover might be BUDGET, NATIONAL; CANCER; CHILD WELFARE; CIVIL RIGHTS; GYMNASTICS; IRELAND, REPUBLIC OF; and LITERARY PRIZES.

Most general yearbooks are put out by encyclopedia publishers. Some are:

1. *Americana Annual*. Grolier, Inc. (1923-date).

2. *Britannica Book of the Year*. Encyclopaedia Britannica, Inc. (1938-date).

3. *World Book Yearbook*. World Book-Childcraft (1962-date).

Subject yearbooks

Yearbooks are also published in specific fields. These yearbooks note annual developments in that field, whether it's law, education, or a medical specialty.

Some yearbooks of current developments are *Year Book of Critical Care Medicine, Year Book of Cancer, Year Book of Human Rights,* and *Yearbook on International Communist Affairs.* Most of these are shelved in libraries with other books on the subject; but since they usually start with the word *yearbook,* they're easy to identify through a library catalog and also in the title volume of *Books in Print.*

Be aware that not all "yearbooks" are really yearbooks. Like all the books discussed previously, they are sometimes other sorts of reference books in disguise.

Old yearbooks

General yearbooks no longer in print are available in large, usually academic, libraries and are often on circulating shelves. The brief sampling below suggests the historical information on general topics (politics, consumer affairs, education, etc.) found within these older volumes:

> *The New International Year Book.* Dodd, Mead & Co. 1907-65. Sample entries from the 1915 volume include BOXING, BRAZIL, DRAMA, EDUCATION IN THE U.S., FOOTBALL, MILITARY PROGRESS,and PHOTOPLAYS (moving pictures). Consider how these articles may read in the yearbook for 1930 or 1960.

Check your library for other old yearbooks such as the *American Year Book; A Record of Events and Progress* (D. Appleton & Co., 1910-50) and *Appleton's Annual Cyclopaedia.* (D. Appleton & Co., 1861-1903).

When you check other reference books in your local library, think of their earlier editions, too. Many of them offer interesting information that you can use in your research.

*   *   *   *

Table 8.1
Selected Subject Encyclopedias

1. *Encyclopaedia Judaica.* 16 vols. Macmillan, 1972.

Covers all areas of Jewish history, religion, philosophy, culture, education, literature, etc.

Sample entries: SABBATH; SABIN, ALBERT BRUCE; SAGES; SASKATCHEWAN; SCHUTZJUDEN.

2. *Encyclopaedia of Religion and Ethics.* Scribner's Sons. 1913-27.

Covers all religions, their ethical systems, customs, philosophies, and related subjects in anthropology, folklore, biology, psychology, economics, sociology, etc.

Sample entries: PROSTITUTION [Greek, Indian, Roman & Semitic]; PUBERTY; QUR'AN; REFORMATION; RELIGIOUS ORDERS.

3. *Encyclopedia of World Art.* 15 vols. McGraw-Hill, 1959-68.

Covers architecture, painting, sculpture, and other art techniques for all countries and periods.

Sample entries: ALASKA; ANDEAN PROTOHISTORY; ARMS and ARMOR; BANTU CULTURES; BAROQUE ART; BASKETRY.

4. *Grzimek's Animal Life Encyclopedia.* 13 vols. Van Nostrand Reinhold, 1972.

Each volume is arranged in chapters and covers a different category of animal: *Insects, Mammals, Birds, Mollusks and Echinoderms,* etc. Includes an index.

Sample entries (from volume on reptiles): ANCIENT REPTILES, GECKOS, LIZARDS, SNAKES, TURTLES, VIPERS.

5. *International Encyclopedia of Education.* 10 vols. Pergamon Press, 1985.

Covers an international perspective of the administrative, political, economic, social, scientific, historical, and contemporary concerns of education.

Sample entries: SCHOOL FINANCE; SELECTION MECHANISMS FOR ENTRY TO HIGHER EDUCATION (by country); SEX DIFFERENCES IN ABILITY AND ACHIEVEMENT; SOUTH AFRICA: SYSTEM OF EDUCATION.

6. *McGraw-Hill Encyclopedia of Science and Technology.* 15 vols. 5th ed. McGraw-Hill, 1982.

Covers all branches of the hard sciences and technology—astronomy, biochemistry, geology, mathematics, physics, and related subjects.

Sample entries: RADIOACTIVE WASTE MANAGEMENT; RADIOCARBON DATING; REMOTE SENSING; REPRODUCTIVE BEHAVIOR; RESPIRATION SYSTEM.

7. *New Catholic Encyclopedia.* 15 vols., with supplements. Publisher's Guild in cooperation with McGraw-Hill. 1967-79.

Covers the structure, history, philosophy, doctrine, and discipline of the Catholic church.

Sample entries: BERGSON, HENRI LOUIS; BRAZILIAN LITERATURE; BUDDHISM; BULLFIGHTING; BYZANTINE ART.

8. *New Grove Dictionary of Music and Musicians.* 20 vols. Macmillan, 1980.

Covers the aesthetics, analysis, history, performing practice, sociology, and theory of music.

Sample entries: ESTERHAZY (family); FERRARA (city); FINLAND; FINGERING (by musical instrument); FLAMENCO; FLUTE.

Several special encyclopedias cover other countries:

9. *Modern Encyclopedia of Russian and Soviet History.* (In progress. Complete to volume 39, Te-Tr.) Academic Press International, 1976- .

10. *Encyclopedia Canadiana.* 10 vols. Grolier of Canada, 1977.

11. *Standard Encyclopaedia of Southern Africa.* 12 vols. Nasou, Ltd. 1970-76.

9
SPECIAL INDEXES

Are you looking for a poem? A song? A speech? A book or film review? How about a fairy tale or a short story?

Short writings are buried in anthologies. You won't find single poems or fairy tales listed in a library's catalog but you will find *books* of poems and fairy tales. You must first determine the title of the book that contains that piece you're after. A special index will help.

BOOK REVIEWS

Book reviews give you a general idea of a book's contents before you bother getting the book itself.

There are more than a dozen book-review indexes covering popular and scholarly books. (If you don't find your book in an index, it may mean that it wasn't reviewed in the magazines the index covers.) Three useful indexes are:

■ *Book Review Index.* Gale Research Co. 1965-date.

Contents. This index locates book reviews published in approximately 200 periodicals published since 1965.

Arrangement. Books are listed under the author's name. There's also a separate title index at the end of each volume, but full information appears under the author entry.

A sample entry reads as follows:

> y HOWE, Norma—*God, The Universe, and Hot Fudge Sundaes.*
> *EJ* - v74 - Ja '85 - p95.
> [y = young adult book; *EJ* = *English Journal.*]

■ *Book Review Digest (BRD).* H.W Wilson Co. 1905-date.

Contents. BRD indexes book reviews in approximately 100 popular and scholarly periodicals from 1905 to date. It also includes summaries of the reviews.

Arrangement. Annual volumes are arranged alphabetically by author. Each volume also includes a subject and title index. To determine the year in which a book was reviewed, check *BRD*'s cumulative author/title index, 1904-74, and annual volumes thereafter.

Abstracts include the word count of the original review (e.g. 500 w). You may prefer selecting the longest ones.

■ *Combined Retrospective Index to Book Reviews in Scholarly Journals, 1886-1974 (CRI).* 15 vols. Carrollton Press. 1979-82.

Contents. This index locates book reviews in approximately 400 scholarly periodicals published between 1886 and 1974, such as *African Affairs, Arizona and the West, Sociology of Education,* and *Polish American Studies.*

Arrangement. CRI provides both an author and a title approach with full bibliographical information appearing under the author's name.

A sample entry:

Gronbech, Vilhelm
The Culture of the Teutons.
Am J Social, v 39 1933-34 p 138
[American Journal of Sociology]

ESSAYS

Essays appear as individual chapters in books and are a useful supplement to periodical articles.

■ *Essay and General Literature Index (EGI).* H. W. Wilson Co. 1900-date.

Contents. EGLI indexes essays published in books since 1900. All subjects from psychology to medicine are represented.

Arrangement. Entries are arranged by author and subject. A sample subject entry looks like this:

MILITARY BASES, AMERICAN
—UNDERDEVELOPED AREAS
Harkavy, R.E. *Military Bases in the Third World. IN The Third World: Premises of U.S. Policy,* ed. by W. S. Thompson. p. 175-200.

FAIRY TALES

■ *Index to Fairy Tales, 1949-72, Including Folklore, Legends and Myths in Collections,* by Norma Ireland. F. W. Faxon Co. 1973; suppl. for 1973-77, 1979.

Contents. This index helps you locate fairy tales, legends, and myths of all nations that have run in anthologies published since 1949.

Arrangement. The index is arranged by subject and title. Full information appears under the title entry. See the key to interpret anthology abbreviations.

Sample entries:

EGRETS [subject]
True Tears

True Tears [story title]
Heady—Safiri p. 46-50

[Heady, Eleanor. *Safiri the Singer: East African Tales.* Follet Publishing Co. 1972.]

FILM REVIEWS

For a broad selection of film reviews that have run in a variety of magazines, check issues of *Reader's Guide to Periodical Literature* under the term MOTION PICTURE REVIEWS—SINGLE WORKS. Also check *Variety Film Reviews, 1907-80* (sixteen volumes) as well as the following:

■ *New York Times Film Reviews.* New York Times/Arno Press. 1913-date.

Contents. The set reproduces in full every film review that has run in *The New York Times* since 1913.

Arrangement. Check either the personal-name index (film star, screenwriter, producer, director, cinematographer, etc.) or the film-title index. Use the cumulative index for 1913-68. After that, indexes appear in the individual volumes.

A sample film entry from the title index looks like this:

> *Home before Dark* 1958, N7, 28:1
> [November 7, 1958, page 28, col 1]

PLAYS

■ *Play Index (PI).* H. W. Wilson. 1949-82.

Contents. PI locates monologues, pantomimes, and one-act and full-length plays published in anthologies and as single volumes.

Arrangement. Plays are listed by author, title, and subject. Full information appears under the author entry and includes a play summary and cast analysis.

Entries look like this:

> Blake, Leila　　　　[playwright entry]
> 　Prey
> 　　Confrontation between would-be blackmailer and wealthy
> 　　Australian homosexual industrialist leads to exchange of
> 　　confidences. 2 m 1 interior
> IN *Can't You Hear Me Talking to You?*
> Homosexuality　　　　　　　　　　　　　[subject entry]
> 　Blake, L. *Prey*

POEMS

There are several indexes to poetry in anthologies. They include the six-volume *Chicorel Index to Poetry in Anthologies and Collections in Print* and *Index to Children's Poetry.* The following is a popular index in libraries:

■ *Poetry Index Annual: A Title, Author, First Line, and Subject Index to Poetry in Anthologies (PIA).* Granger Book Co., 1982-date.

Content. PIA now updates *Granger's Index to Poetry* regularly. It locates thousands of poems in hundreds of poetry anthologies. Previous editions of Granger's are still useful in finding older poems.

Arrangement. Poems are arranged by title, author, first line, and subject. Anthology abbreviations are spelled out in the key.

A sample entry:

```
Dogs          [subject]
    Dog's death. John Updike. POT.
    [POT = Poetspeak Bradbury Press, 1983.]
"It snowed/all that day."          [First line]
    Depth of field. Agnes McDonald. FOR.
    [FOR = Four North Carolina Women Poets. St. Andrews Press, 1982.]
```

SHORT STORIES

■ *Short Story Index (SSI).* H. W. Wilson. 1953-date.

Contents. SSI includes short stories in over 4,500 short-story anthologies and magazines published since the early 1950s. Some magazines currently covered are *Atlantic, Ms., Parents Magazine, Redbook, Rolling Stone,* and *Sports Illustrated.*

Arrangement. Stories are filed by author, title, and subject. Full information appears under the author entry.

Sample entries look like this:

```
Jackson, Shirley          [author]
    Lottery          [story title]
        Sullivan, N. comp. The Treasury of American Short Stories. Wolf, L.
        ed. Wolf's Complete Book of Terror.
```

SONGS

■ *Popular Song Index.* Scarecrow Press. 1975; suppl. 1978.

Contents. This index locates folk songs, hymns, pop tunes, sea chanteys, etc. in over 350 songbooks published since 1940.

Arrangement. Songs are arranged by title and first line with separate composer and lyricist indexes.

A sample title entry looks like this:

```
"The Pause of Mister Clause" Arlo Guthrie. FL:
        Why do you set there so strange. 115. [The phrase in quotes is the
        song title. FL = first line. Book no. 115 = This Is the Arlo Guthrie Book.
        NY: Amsco Music Pub., 1969]
```

■ *Song Index (SI).* H. W. Wilson. 1926; suppl., 1934. Reprinted by Shoe String Press. 1966. (The Shoe String Press edition includes two volumes in one. Look for the supplement at the end of the volume.)

Contents. SI indexes 19,000 American and foreign-language songs that appeared in 281 songbooks published before 1934.

Arrangement. SI lists song by first line, composer, author, and title.

Look for the full anthology citation in the abbreviations key. A first-line entry looks like this:

"Love was once a little boy." J.A. Wade. HSE 3. [HSE3 = Hatton, J.L., & Faning, E. *The Songs of England.* 3 v. Boosey n.d.]

SPEECHES

■ *Speech Index: An Index to Collections of World Famous Orations and Speeches for Various Occasions, 1935-1965 (SI).* suppl. 1966-80. 4th ed. Scarecrow Press.

Contents. SI locates contemporary and centuries-old speeches made by a variety of speakers from George Jessel to Martin Luther, published in 115 books and anthologies.

Arrangement. Speeches are arranged alphabetically by subject and orator.

Sample entries:

GELL-MANN, MURRAY   [subject]
Walter, I.

Presentation [of the Nobel Prize for Physics to Murray Gell-Mann, 1969].
NOLPH 4:294

[*Nobel Lectures: Physics, 1901-1970.* 4 v. Elsevier, 1967-72].

Indexes cover almost every subject and help you locate anything from pictures of sculpture (in *Sculpture Index*) to houses illustrated in books such as *A Country House Index: An Index to Over 2,000 Country Houses Illustrated in 107 Books . . . Published Between 1715 and 1872.* Some indexes are not really indexes; rather they're reference books that use the word *index* in their titles. Though there's no current source that identifies all indexes of every type, they're all potential sources for ferreting out information buried in other publications.

10
RESEARCHING IN NEWSPAPERS

Are newspapers really research tools? Indeed they are. Newspapers are time capsules, freeze-frames of life as it existed in a certain time and place. Their ads give us the cost of consumer goods; their photos show us clothing styles; their classified ads reveal economic conditions; their editorials discuss the politic mood. Newspapers of specific cities and countries mention people and events that may not be covered in great detail in other reference resources. The fine points of people's lives are grist for the writer's mill.

THE KEY TO BURIED INFORMATION

You can use newspapers for the flavor of the times. Or you can look for a particular fact or event, such as your great-grandfather's obituary or the news of last year's city scandal. To find specific events within the pages of a newspaper, you must use a newspaper index.

Newspaper indexes vary in form and coverage. Some are typed on file cards by the staff of a community library and cover only local news. Others, like those of the *Washington Post* and *The New York Times*, cover national, international, and local news; are issued in book form; and are sold by subscription to large libraries.

National Newspaper Index (Information Access Corp.) is a new kind of newspaper index. On microfilm, it jointly indexes the last three years of five newspapers— *The New York Times*, *The Christian Science Monitor*, the *Wall Street Journal*, the *Los Angeles Times*, and the *Washington Post*. (These newspapers are also indexed individually in print form.) This type of index is a time-saver because it interfiles several years of several newspapers.

WHO COLLECTS NEWSPAPERS?

Almost every city and town has a newspaper, and almost every local library saves it. Firms like Bell & Howell have microfilmed hundreds of community newspapers, but only the largest libraries collect more than a selection of them. Libraries don't have the space for many newspapers, nor do they have the demand to justify their expense.

Libraries needn't own every newspaper in any case. You can usually get information from any newspaper anywhere by writing to the public library in that community.

CLIPPING SERVICES AND NEWS DIGESTS

News digests summarize major news events. Clipping services compile and package articles from dozens, even hundreds of newspapers that libraries normally do not buy individually. Many of their published cumulations are in large libraries. Some of these collections are as follows.

American news

1. *Editorials on File*. Facts on File, Inc. 1970-date. Also comes in microform. Monthly.

   Each month, a 125-page booklet summarizes newspaper editorials on about ten major news topics, such as the president's tax-reform plan, the death of Karen Ann Quinlan, spying in the Navy, terrorism abroad, racism in South Africa, and the New York City subway vigilante shooting of 1985.

   Editorials are reprinted from one to two dozen American newspapers of the 150 or so covered and represent varying points of view.

2. *NewsBank*. NewsBank, Inc. 1970-date. On microfiche only. Quarterly.

   About 200 newspapers from over 130 American cities have been clipped, rearranged, and microfilmed according to fourteen topics ranging from consumer affairs and social relations to environment and health. (Separate sets cover film and TV, fine arts and architecture, literature, and the performing arts.) Because of the many newspapers included, *NewsBank* allows you to see a regional perspective of national issues.

   Start with *NewsBank*'s printed subject and name indexes to find the articles on microfiche.

International news

1. *Facts on File: World News Digest with Index (FOF)*. Facts on File, Inc. 1941-date. Weekly.

   FOF summarizes major foreign and American news events in sports, space, the environment, religion, economics, the arts, etc.

2. *ISLA: Information Services on Latin America*. Oakland, Calif. 1970-date. Monthly.

   ISLA reproduces clips from seven major American newspapers and two British newspapers on such Latin American concerns as civil rule in Guatemala, Salvadorean troop movements, corruption in Brazil's military regime, and oil in Colombia.

3. *Keesing's Contemporary Archives: Record of World Events*. Longman

Group, Ltd., London. 1931-date. (Also comes in microform). Weekly.

Keesing's analyzes worldwide political and economic events from assassinations, coups, and strikes to treaties and elections. It has discussed such topics as relations between North and South Korea, the general elections in Singapore, and Mexico's economic situation. The index is arranged by country, then subdivided by major subject.

News from abroad

Views expressed in the foreign press often differ from those found in American newspapers. Since foreign newspaper subscriptions are in short supply in most libraries, digests of them are extremely useful.

1. *African Recorder: a Fortnightly Record of African Events*. New Delhi: Recorder Press. 1962-date. Biweekly.

   The *African Recorder* digests news largely from such African and Asian newspapers as the New Delhi *Patriot* and the Baghdad *Observer*, periodicals, radio broadcasts, embassies, and government sources in that part of the world.

   It covers topics from the South African education crisis and tribal violence in Uganda to women's rights in Algeria.

2. *Asian Recorder: Weekly Digest of Asian Events*. New Delhi: Recorder Press 1955-date. Weekly.

   The *Asian Recorder* gathers its information from many of the same sources as the *African Recorder*, reporting on such news as the diminishing tiger population in Nepal, China's criticism of Marxism, and fighting in Beirut.

3. *Canadian News Facts: The Indexed Digest of Canadian Current Events (CNF)*. Marpep Publishing Ltd. 1967-date. Biweekly.

   CNF summarizes stories from news agencies and twenty of Canada's leading newspapers. Stories cover anything from the nation's jobless rate and the school funding bill in Ontario to Canadian opinion of the U. S. Star Wars defense plan.

4. *Current Digest of the Soviet Press (CDSP)*. American Association for the Advancement of Slavic Studies. 1947-date. Weekly.

   CDSP translates a selection of articles from Soviet newspapers such as *Pravda* and *Izvestia* and some magazines. Topics might cover Soviet boxing, sex education on television for teens, school reform, and *Pravda's* interpretation of Premier Gorbachev's interview by *Time* magazine.

5. *Foreign Broadcast Information Service (FBIS)*. *Daily Report*. Issued by the National Technical Information Service. 1978-date. Also comes on microform.

FBIS reports news from China, Latin America, Eastern Europe, and the Soviet Union reprinted from press agencies, television broadcasts, newspapers, and government statements. Topics may cover anything from the latest territorial issue between two nations to a recent drought.

NEWS FROM OLD NEWSPAPERS

You already know that old newspapers can help you dig out forgotten facts and reconstruct the atmosphere of a past period. A New York newspaper published during the War of 1812 will provide authentic detail for your historical work of that era.

You have access to many newspapers in microform through interlibrary loan. One historic collection of newspapers comes in book form. It's called the *Great Contemporary Issues Series* (Ayer Publishing Co.). The series consists of thirty-plus volumes of article reprints from *The New York Times* as early as the 1860s. Each volume in the set covers a particular subject.

Your novel on business tycoons may benefit from an overview of actual history as it was portrayed in a major newspaper.

The volume entitled *Big Business*, for example, starts its coverage with 1866 discussions of the tyranny of corporations and traces the growth of industry to the mid 1970s.

The volume called *Popular Culture* demonstrates America's popular taste through actual newspaper coverage of vaudeville, radio, early talking pictures, television, etc. It includes reviews of popular books, plays, movies, musical performances, and television programs as well as interviews with performers and authors from 1900 to the mid 1970s.

Other titles in the series cover China, labor and management, terrorism, black Africa, Central America and the Caribbean, the cities, energy and environment, crime and justice, drugs, education in the United States, ethnic groups in American life, food and population, Japan, the mass media and politics, the Middle East, medicine and health care, the presidency, religion in America, sports and society, values Americans live by, and women and their changing roles.

Look for all volumes in the series in a reference book called *Books in Series*.

Many newspapers in microform have been gathered into subject sets and sold to large libraries. Check your local libraries for the collections named below. Most have no indexes to the individual articles in the newspapers, but you can use them by time period, region, and coverage of particular historical events.

1. *Canadian Newspapers on Microfilm*. Canadian Library Association. Includes more than 300 nineteenth and twentieth-century Canadian newspapers.

2. *Civil War Newspapers on Microfilm*. Bell & Howell.
   Includes 301 newspapers representing thirty Union and Confederate towns and cities in thirty-three states and territories published between 1861 and 1865.

3. *Contemporary Newspapers of the North American Indian*. Bell & Howell.

   Includes forty-nine newspapers from the 1960s and 1970s covering twenty-three states and the District of Columbia.

4. *Early American Newspapers, 1704-1820*. Readex Microprint.
   Includes all existing newspapers listed in Clarence Brigham's *History and Bibliography of American Newspapers, 1690-1820*. The newspapers come from twenty-nine states and the District of Columbia.

5. *Negro Newspapers on Microfilm*. Library of Congress.
   Includes complete and partial files for most of the 200 well-known black American newspapers covering the mid 1800s to the mid 1900s.

6. *The Newspapers of Ireland*. Memo Ltd., Dublin, distributed in the United States by Bell & Howell.
   Includes twenty-five Irish newspapers from the nineteenth and early twentieth century.

BORROWING NEWSPAPERS

If your library doesn't have any of the newspaper microfilm collections mentioned above, consider borrowing newspapers individually on interlibrary loan. They're recorded by title in two standard reference books: *Newspapers in Microform: U.S., 1948-72* (and supplements) and *Newspapers in Microform: Foreign Countries, 1948-72* (and supplements).

If you want to borrow a Kentucky newspaper of 1898, for example, check *Newspapers in Microform: U.S. 1948-72* under KENTUCKY, and scan the list by city for a newspaper that falls into the time period you need.

The codes at the bottom of each entry list the U. S. libraries that own the newspaper in microform and may lend them.

WHAT ABOUT NEWSPAPER LIBRARIES?

When you borrow newspapers or request information from them, you'll most often approach libraries. Many newspaper libraries are not open to the public, although they may continue to handle some mail or phone queries. In any event, many newspapers have ceased publication. The only place you can find them is in community libraries.

Ayer Directory of Publications names current newspapers in the United States. Clarence Brigham's *History and Bibliography of American Newspa-*

pers, 1690-1820 and *American Newspapers, 1821-1936* by Winifred Gregory document past newspapers.

The *American Library Directory* (R. R. Bowker Co.) will identify public and academic libraries nationwide to whom you can write for information.

Studies have shown that most people read only a small portion of their daily newspaper. When you have the chance to see a newspaper that is twenty-five or more years old, you'll see it differently. And you'll probably read it from cover to cover.

11
GOVERNMENT "DOCUMENTS"

If you were to name the largest publisher in the country, the United States government might be the last name to come to mind. Yet it's true. Uncle Sam generates thousands of publications each year, far more than the output of the largest commercial publisher.

Government "documents' include far more than official papers, hearings, and committee reports. The government publishes many things: cookbooks, national-park guides, posters, employment directories, dictionaries, magazines, indexes, bibliographies, directories, maps, handbooks, histories, textbooks, exhibition catalogs—just about everything that commercial publishers issue except for fiction. The subjects cover health, consumerism, economics, agriculture, the military, etc., and parallel the government's concerns as represented by its various departments (Department of the Interior, Department of Transportation, etc.), their subdivisions, and outside contractors. A government "document" is nothing more than a publication printed at government expense.

Recipes for Quantity Service, a card file of recipes issued for military cooks by the Armed Forces Recipe Service, is a government document because it is published by the Department of Defense—at government expense. Other documents are the *ZIP Code Directory*, issued by the U.S. Postal Service; the *West Point Catalog*, issued by the U.S. Military Academy; and *American Education*, a magazine issued by the Department of Education that accepts articles from freelance writers.

DOCUMENT DIVERSITY

The list below shows the diversity of documents that come from the many departments, bureaus, agencies, and subagencies of the federal government.

Publications for consumers and taxpayers

- *No More Butts: A Guide to Quitting Smoking.* Issued by the Public Health Service, Department of Health and Human Services. [1983?] 1 p.

- *Social Security and Case Tips.* Issued by the Social Security Administration, Department of Health and Human Services. 1980. 5 pp.

Posters

- *Voyager at Saturn*. Issued by the National Aeronautics and Space Administration. 1981.

- *Cloud Code Chart*. Issued by the Department of Commerce. 1978.

Pamphlets and brochures

- *Operation Awareness: State to State: A Report on Efforts to Reduce Fraud, Waste, and Abuse in Food Stamp Program*. Issued by the Food and Nutrition Service, Department of Agriculture. 1983. 8 pp.

- *Bank Capital Trends and Financing*. Issued by the Federal Reserve Bank. 1983. 19 pp.

Bibliographies

- *Antarctic Bibliography*. Prepared by the Library of Congress by the Division of Polar Programs, National Science Foundation. 1965-date. Irregularly published.

- *Alcohol/Safety Public Information Materials: Catalog #6*. Issued by the National Highway and Traffic Safety Administration, Department of Transportation. 1983. 234 pp.

Directories and guidebooks

- *Detailed Listing of Real Property Owned by the United States and Used by the Department of Defense for Military Functions throughout the World*. Issued by the General Services Administration. Annual.

- *Directory: Federal, State and Local Government Consumer Officers*. Issued by the Office of Consumer Affairs, Department of Health and Human Services. Annual.

Handbooks and manuals

- *Attack Helicopter Team Handbook*. Issued by the Department of the Army. 1983. 88 pp.

- *A Manual for Using Energy Analysis for Plant Siting: Report to the Nuclear Regulatory Commission*. Issued by National Technical Information Services? 1983. 1 v.

Dictionaries and glossaries

- *Dictionary of Alaska Place Names*. Issued by the Geological Survey Department of the Interior. 1967. 1,084 pp.

- *Dictionary of Basic Military Terms: A Soviet View.* Issued by the Department of the Air Force. 1976 256 pp.

Magazines

- *Talking Book Topics.* Issued by National Library Services for the Blind and Physically Handicapped, Library of Congress. 1935-date. Bimonthly.

- *Business America.* Issued by the Department of Commerce. 1978-date. Biweekly.

Indexes and abstracts

- *Diabetes Literature Index.* Issued by the National Institute of Arthritis, Diabetes, and Digestive and Kidney Diseases, Department of Health and Human Services. 1966-date. Monthly.

- *Computer Program Abstracts.* Issued by National Aeronautics and Space Administration. 1969-date.

Hearings

- *Profile of Organized Crime, Mid-Atlantic Region: Hearings before the Permanent Subcommittee on Investigations of the Committee on Governmental Affairs, United States Senate, 48th Congress, 1st Session, February 15, 23 & 24, 1983.* 506 pp.

WHO COLLECTS GOVERNMENT DOCUMENTS?

Documents defined by law as having educational value and of public interest are distributed without cost to more than 1,300 U.S. libraries. Libraries designated as depository libraries include each state library and most large public and academic libraries.

The documents sent to depository libraries are a fraction of the total output. Many of the 25,000-plus titles published annually are scientific reports and technical publications with limited public appeal. The heaviest user of government reports, in fact, is not the general public. It's state and local governments and companies that do business with the government.

Nevertheless, depository libraries make many documents available to the public.

HOW TO FIND DOCUMENTS

The government and several commercial publishers issue indexes and bibliographies to help you identify potentially useful documents. Before diving in, however, you must know the idiosyncrasies of documents so you can find them. Their unusual features concern the way they're cataloged and the way they're shelved.

Documents are not classified according to the Dewey Decimal or the Library of Congress subject system. They follow a system of their own—the Superintendent of Documents, or Sudocs, system—which results in a call number like this:

D 1.57:981

The first letter, in most cases, stands for the issuing agency. *D* stands for the Department of Defense, *I* stands for the Interior Department; *T*, the Treasury Department, etc. The other numbers in the Sudocs number represent types of publications, like handbooks and annual reports. Sometimes a volume number or part of a year is included.

Since documents are shelved according to issuing agency rather than by subject, they're not easy to browse. Furthermore, each government agency does not publish material in one subject alone. The Department of Defense, for example, issues a training manual for aviation boatswain's mates; an introduction to FORTRAN, a computer language; and the recipe cards for Army cooks mentioned in the beginning of this chapter.

The unique cataloging and shelving systems that documents use are the reasons they're kept in a separate department of the library. Though the separation has led to a mystique about documents, it arose for purely practical reasons.

Because you can't shelf-browse government documents, you must identify them through certain finding tools.

DOCUMENTS-FINDING TOOLS

Many documents are now available in microform. They include not only recently published documents but also decades-old, out-of-print, nondepository items formerly unavailable in depository libraries. Many of these have been microfilmed and repackaged as sets.

These microform sets of documents come with multivolume indexes in print form. More libraries own the indexes to documents than the collections of documents they cover. Due to the high cost of the collections and the heavy duplication of microfilmed materials among them, many libraries have purchased some jointly with other libraries and share them through interlibrary loan.

If you want to write about any of such diverse topics as eavesdropping in industry, nuclear-waste dumping, the progress made in conquering cancer, children in pornography, ballistic-missile systems, the history of atomic-bomb testing in the United States, or the military applications of lasers, government publications will provide you with much information. You'll find it through the indexes and finding tools that follow.

1. *Monthly Catalog (MC)*. Issued by the Superintendent of Documents. 1895-date. (Latest five years comes on microfilm.)

Contents. MC is a bibliography of government books, magazines, brochures, pamphlets, and reports. Though it's the major source for identifying documents, it actually includes less than half the federal output. It excludes documents that government contractors forget to send to Washington for recording in the MC and countless technical reports that are mentioned in indexes of their own.

Items marked with a black dot are distributed to documents libraries. Those that include a stock number (S/N) and a price are for sale.

Arrangement. Items in the MC are not in alphabetical or subject order. They're arranged by issuing agency (Department of the Interior, Heritage Conservation and Recreation Service, etc.). Since you'll normally use the subject approach, start with the cumulative subject indexes or the index in the back of monthly volumes. For anything published prior to 1971, check item #2 below.

Entries in *MC*'s subject index look like this:

DWELLING—UNITED STATES
>   *Farm and home foreclosures: hearing before the Sub-committee on Courts of the Committee on the Judiciary, United States Senate, Ninety-eighth Congress, First session, on farm and home foreclosures and related personal bankruptcies, March 14, 1983,* 83-23231

EARTHQUAKE PREDICTION
>   *Prediction of earthquake response spectra,* 83-22546

Another helpful way to identify documents is to use the title-keyword index appearing in the back of each volume since July, 1980. It looks like this:

China's economy and foreign trade/	83-21765
cholesterol reference method/, The Procedure for	83-22400

Keywords are aligned at the left. The title begins reading after the slash mark. Use the number—83-22400—to see the publication's completed citation and Sudocs number within the volume.

2. *Cumulative Subject Index to the Monthly Catalog of United States Government Publications, 1900-71.* 15 vols. Carrollton Press. Comes with a microfilm collection of documents.

Contents. This index includes all titles listed in the MC from 1900 to 1971. The *Cumulative Subject Index* saves time by offering one look-up point instead of up to seventy-two.

Arrangement. Titles from all seventy-two annual issues of MC are interfiled into one alphabet. Each entry is shortened, so you must refer back to the particular annual volume of the MC for the complete citation (number of pages, issuing agency, Sudocs call number, etc.) Listings in the *Cumulative Subject Index* look like this:

RADIO WAVES
    radio polarimetry at sea, USSR study   (70) 1995
    [(70) = the 1970 volume of *MC*: 1995 = item # 1995]
RAFTS
    navigation of waterways by   (25) 723
RAILROAD EMPLOYEES
    Women -
during and after World War II   (45) 302

3. *Cumulative Title Index to United States Public Documents, 1789-1976*. 16 vols. United States Historical Documents Insititute. Comes with a microform set of documents.

Contents. This index includes all titles listed in the *MC* from 1895 to 1976 and several of its predecessors. If you have a document title but no date or Sudocs number, the *Cumulative Title Index* will help you find it quickly. Otherwise, its usefulness as a title-only approach is somewhat limited.

Arrangement. The index interfiles document titles into a single alphabet.

Entries look like this:

Eagle killing in Wyoming, hearings, 1971 Y4.Ap6/2:P91
    [Issued by the Senate Appropriations Committee]
Earth vibrations caused by quarry blasting, 1937
    I28.23:3353. [Issued by the Dept. of Interior]
Ecology of space flight, USSR, 1961. Y3.J66:13/94
    [Issued by Joint Publications Research Service]

4. *Government Printing Office (GPO) Sales Publications Reference File*. Issued by the Superintendent of Documents. 1977-date.

Contents. Called *PRF* for short, this file is a books-in-print to government documents. It contains only the for-sale items that are mentioned in the *MC*. (*MC* also includes titles that are not for sale.)

Arrangement. The file comes in microfiche (four-by-six inch cards of microfilm).

The approach to the *PRF* is by keyword or key phrase, subject, title, series, and personal author. Sample entries are:

Defense procurement   [subject]
Defense spending and the economy   [title]
DeGroot Rodney C.   [author]

5. *Index to United States Government Periodicals*. Infordata International, Inc. Quarterly. 1970-date.

Contents. This index covers approximately 170 magazines published by Uncle Sam for chaplains; military lawyers; government employees in public health, gerontology, consumerism, education, energy, etc.

Arrangement. Articles are arranged alphabetically by subject. Examples follow.

> FEDERAL BUREAU OF INVESTIGATION
> > *Interstate identification index.* Emmet A. Rathbun, il, ref FBI Law Enf Bul 54 1 14-17 Ja 85-044
> > [FBI Law Enforcement Bulletin, vol. 54, no. 1, p. 14-17, Jan. 85.044 is the order number for libraries who wish to order the magazine in microform]
> FERRARO, GERALDINE A.
> > *Profile of the 1984 elections.* Elizabeth Yadlosky, il Cong Res Serv Rev 6 1 2-5+ Ja 85-314
> > [Congressional Research Service Review]
> FIJI
> > *Fiji: a profile.* Dept. Sta Bul 85 2094 31 Ja 85-029

6. *Public Affairs Information Service (PAIS) Bulletin.* Public Affairs Information Service, Inc. Biweekly. 1915-date.

Contents. PAIS is a commerical periodical index that covers select government reports of political and social significance from cocaine use in Hollywood to the bribery of union officials.

Unlike *MC,* which is a bibliography, *PAIS* is an index. It indexes the articles in many government periodicals and serial publications. As a bibliography, *MC* indexes magazine titles, not the articles in them.

For example, the 1982 issue of *MC* shows little in the subject index under Ronald Reagan's name. In *PAIS* for that same period, however, there are countless references to him in government serial publications, particularly documenting his speeches reprinted there.

Arrangement. PAIS is arranged by subject. Most entries for government publications start with the words *United States,* as in the following entry:

> HEALTH SERVICES
> > United States. Senate. Com. on Agric., Nutrition, and Forestry.
> > *Emerging issues in the delivery of rural health services.* '84 vi + 80 p bibls tables charts (98th Cong., 2d sess.) (S. print 98-239) (Com. print) pa

7. *CIS/Index and Abstracts to Publications of the U.S. Congress.* Congressional Information Service, Inc. 1970-date. Comes with a microform set of documents.

Contents. This CIS set contains abstracts of all congressional publications—hearings, prints, reports, press releases, etc.

Though congressional publications also appear in the *MC,* CIS coverage is more detailed because it indexes articles, chapters, and other parts of documents. It also includes far more subject approaches than the *MC* and provides a summary of each item listed.

Arrangement. You can look up information by subject, witness, corporation or company name, subcommittee, popular names of bills, laws, and reports. Entries look like this:

> END WORLD HUNGER, INC.   [corporation]
> *Hunger problem review and food assistance programs improvement*
> *proposals,*
>   H161-52.6
> ENDEAN, STEPHEN R.   [witness]
> *Acquired immune deficiency syndrome, Fed response,*
>   H401-82
> ENERGY CONSERVATION IN BUILDINGS   [subject]
> *Air pollution indoors, overview,*
>   H701-32.4

Match the accession number in the index volume (e.g., H161-52.6) with its entry in the abstract volume for a summary. The abstract volume also gives the Sudocs number, so you can borrow the publication.

CIS, Inc. has also filmed retrospective congressional publications in other sets. See items 8-10.

8. *CIS/U.S. Congressional Committee Prints Index from the Earliest Publications through 1969.* Congressional Information Service, Inc. Comes with a microform set of documents.

Congressional committee prints can help you research many issues, from a history of postal rate changes to the concerns of the U.S. fishing industry.

Congress spends much time in hearings, committees, and subcommittees. Many of their deliberations result in proposed legislation. Committee prints are background studies of an issue under investigation.

The prints provide more in-depth data than are generally given through witness testimony in Congressional hearings. Much of the information is not found in other documents.

Since congressional committee prints are internal working papers, they're printed in small quantities and not distributed to the public except by request. They may range from a few pages to a few volumes in length. Until recently, depository libraries did not receive most of them, nor were they sold by the Government Printing Office.

The following is a selection from the *Prints Index* by subject:

> RELIGIOUS LIBERTY
> *Communism, church and state under.* vol. 7: Cuba
>   (89/1/65) S0743
>   [89th Congress first session, 1965. S0743 = Senate print number
>   0743]

REPATRIATION
  Displaced persons, problem of, preliminary study for field survey
  (80/1/47) H4629
RHODE ISLAND
  Alcohol, interstate traffic in intoxicating liquors. Laws of various
  states relating to
  (62/3/13) H2764

9. *CIS/U.S. Congressional Committee Hearings Index, Early 1800s-1969.*
Congressional Information Service, Inc. Comes with a microform set of
documents.

Contents. Hearings—investigations conducted prior to final action on
a piece of legislation—include testimony by prominent and newsworthy
people, from film stars and educators to labor leaders and business execu-
tives. Topics concern anything from educational broadcasting to French
and British membership in the European Defense Community.

Arrangement. The index includes separate volumes for the names of
witnesses testifying before a congressional committee hearing, together
with a subject arrangement of hearings topics.

Some entries from the 1953-58 name and subject indexes are as follows:

Name Index
  FAULKNER, J.W.
    Polygamist community and its impact on children
      in Short Creek, Ariz, investigation
      (84) S1139-1-D
      [84th Congress, Senate print no. 1139-1-D]
  KANELOS, GUS
    Labor racketeering in Pittsburgh, Pa, area, investigation
    (83) H1458-3

Subject Index
  BELMONT HOSIERY MILLS
    Textile industry problems, review
    (85) S1302-1-C
  BOULDER PEACE COUNCIL
    Communist activities in Ohio area, investigation
    (84) H1505-9

10. *CIS Serial Set Index, 1789-1969.* Congressional Information Service,
Inc. Comes with a microform set of documents.

Contents. Writers will find the *Serial Set* unparalleled for tracing the
background of various issues in American history—the history of different immigrant groups, child labor, women's suffrage, and the development of social security, to name some. Dee Brown, author of *Bury My
Heart at Wounded Knee* (Holt, Rinehart & Winston), used the *Serial Set*
heavily in researching *Wounded Knee* and the nearly two dozen other
books he wrote on the American Indians.

There are four types of congressional publications: hearings, prints, reports, and documents (used as a publication title, not in the descriptive sense). Hearings and prints have already been discussed. Reports and documents are part of the *Serial Set.*

Congressional reports provide added information on a matter being considered as a bill. They are essential to the legislative process.

Documents normally are not essential to this process. They're miscellaneous publications that fit no other category. For example, they include annual reports from nongovernmental organizations—corporations, foundations, societies, symphony orchestras, commissions, and councils such as the Boy Scouts of America and the American Legion. These groups are required by law to submit their annual reports to Congress. The SEC, for example, requires full disclosure from public corporations to protect the public against unlawful practices in the securities industry. For this purpose, they request copies of corporate annual reports.

The *Serial Set* has generated more than a third of a million publications since it began in the late eighteenth century. Some libraries own part of the set in hard copy. The entire group of publications to 1969, however, is now available in this microform set.

Arrangement. Volumes are arranged by year and keyword.

The following is a selection from the 1857-79 volume of the *Serial Set Index:*

OWYHEE
> *Military post of Camp Three Forks, Owyhee, Idaho Territory* H.exdoc.
> 174 (42-2) 1513
> [House executive document 174; 42nd Congress, 2d session, item
> no. 1513]
PACIFIC RAILROAD
> *Construction of railroad to Pacific Ocean* H. misdoc. 47 (36-1) 1065
PAROLE
> *Paroles granted to rebel officers* H.exdoc. 57 (37-3) 1162

11. *Declassified Documents Reference System, Research Publications.* 1975-date. Comes with a microform set of documents.

Contents. The set includes formerly top-secret documents—cabinet meeting minutes, correspondence, reports, etc.—that have been sanitized according to the Privacy Act of 1974.

Much of the information in the set covers foreign governments—from biographies of their leaders prepared by the CIA to reports on hot spots around the globe. Much-discussed topics include atomic weapons and disarmament, biological warfare, POW's, and the USSR.

Arrangement. Check the subject index in each volume. Refer to the abstract volume for a summary of a group of documents.

COMMERCIALLY PUBLISHED
DOCUMENT-FINDING TOOLS

There are other ways to identify certain government publications if you're not near a depository library that owns the finding tools previously discussed. There are several commercially published subject bibliographies listing government-published dictionaries, atlases, handbooks, pamphlets, books, bibliographies, indexes, etc.

You can borrow these bibliographies as well as many of the documents they name through interlibrary loan. To find the bibliographies, check *SGBIP* under *United States—Government Publications—Bibliography*. Some are:

1. *A Bibliography of United States Government Bibliographies, 1974-76* by Roberta Scull. Pierian Press. 1979.

This bibliography names subject bibliographies published by the government. It's arranged by broad category and includes a subject index.

2. *Government Reference Books*. 1968/69-date. Published every two years by Libraries Unlimited.

Covers pamphlets, books, bibliographies, directories, and other government publications in all subjects. It's arranged by broad category with separate subject and title indexes.

3. *Guide to U.S. Government Directories, 1970-1980* by Donna Rae Larson. Oryx Press. 1981.

Lists only directories published by the government on all topics, such as divorce records listings, educational opportunities, and endangered species. Arranged by Sudocs call number. Use the index to find directories by subject.

4. *New Guide to Popular Government Publications for Libraries and Home Reference* by Walter Newsome. Libraries Unlimited. 1978.

Covers a wide range of government publications books and pamphlets in consumer and business subjects—Eskimo arts and crafts, export opportunities, proper and improper use of drugs, the benefits of space exploration, mulch tilling, first aid, Native American civil rights, etc.

You may also want to check a quarterly publication called *U.S. Government Books: Recent Releases*. It's available by subscription or you can check a library's copy.

HOW TO GET THE DOCUMENTS YOU NEED

You've identified a group of government documents you'd like to see. After you've checked the library shelves to see if the library owns them, ask to borrow them through interlibrary loan in either the print or microform version.

Documents are far from stodgy and dull affairs of state. They're the living history of this country and vital in many writing projects.

12
WHO'S WHO?

People research is intriguing, whether you're tracing a contemporary celebrity or a historical figure. You'll deal with people's perceptions of others and contradictions that appear in print. Biographical research will test your skills of intuition to the limit—once you find the information, that is.

Biographical research would be simple if every person on whom we want information were conveniently listed in *Who's Who*. Unfortunately, they're not. *Who's Who* is like *Reader's Guide*. It doesn't include everything or everyone. Academic libraries may own between 500 and 1,000 recent and old who's who dictionaries. *Who's Who* is actually the title of one particular book. It lists approximately 32,000 current people worldwide and is hardly the answer to all your biographical problems.

Not every biographical dictionary (BD) starts with the words *Who's Who*—one example is *Biographical Dictionary of English Architects*. Nor are all BDs general. Some of them list people by country. (*Who's Who in Finland*), profession (*Who's Who in American Education*), or era (*American Authors, 1600-1900*). Many are issued annually (*Who's Who in the East*), or they were published only once. They may include prominent people or lesser known individuals. You'll find many in large libraries, others in select or regional libraries only.

Many BDs are not what they seem. Some are vanity books assembled mainly to sell to the people listed; others are membership rosters for organizations such as *Who's Who in Art Materials*.

The sheer number of BDs presents awesome choices for any researcher. Where do you begin?

MASTER INDEXES TO BIOGRAPHICAL DICTIONARIES (BDs)

How much biographical information do you need? If it's just a point or two about a person's life, BDs may be sufficient. Entries usually include basic data and vital statistics such as date of birth; names of parents, spouse, and children; education and degrees; career highlights; and awards.

The question is, which BD should you check? Suppose you needed some information about John Ehrlichman, former Nixon administration official.

Many people, like Ehrlichman, appear in more than one BD. If you randomly hunt through BDs and find an entry in *Who's Who in America*, you're likely to stop your search not realizing that Ehrlichman is also listed in several other BDs. Much of the information in BDs is standard, but some BDs offer new, different, or conflicting facts, so it pays to check more than one.

To find information in BDs, use a biographical master index (BMI). BMIs interfile all names found in up to 500 different BDs into a single alphabet. They tell, through abbreviations, which BDs include information on any person listed.

A BMI entry looks like this:

> Ehrlichman, John Daniel 1925-
> BlueB76, IntWW 79, -80, WhoAm80

The abbreviations stand for the *Blue Book*, 1976; *International Who's Who*, 1979 and 1980; and *Who's Who in America*, 1980.

The following list of BMIs includes those published by Gale Research Co. You should become acquainted with them.

1. *Biography and Genealogy Master Index*. Eight-volume base set and three-volume supplement. 1980-81. Also in a microform version, *Bio-base*, 1978-date.

In large libraries, start your search with this BMI. You'll find a complete list of BDs that each BMI covers on the book's inside front and back covers.

The individual volumes listed below (#2 - #7) are incorporated into this large set. You'll find the specific BMIs in departments or special libraries according to their subject. The performing arts BMI, for example, would be in a theater arts library.

2. *Author Biographies Master Index*. 2 vols. 2d ed. 1984.
Interfiles the names from 140 BDs such as *Female Poets of America*, *Dictionary of Oriental Literatures*, and *Minnesota Writers*.

3. *Children's Authors and Illustrators*. 3rd ed. 1981.
Interfiles the names from about 200 BDs such as *Canada Writers*, *Catholic Authors*, and *Newbery Medal Books*.

4. *Historical Biographical Dictionaries Master Index*. 1980.
Interfiles the names from about three dozen BDs such as *Biographical Dictionary of American Educators*, *Dictionary of American Religious Biography*, and *Who's Who of the Colored Race*.

5. *Journalist Biographies Master Index*. 1979.
Interfiles the names from about 200 BDs such as *American Radical Press*, *Famous War Correspondents*, and *Investigative Journalists*.

6. *Performing Arts Biography Master Index.* 2d ed. 1982.

Interfiles the names from about 100 BDs such as *Black American Playwrights, The Dance Encyclopedia,* and *The Movie Makers.*

7. *Writers for Young Adults: Biographies Master Index.* 1979.

Interfiles the names from about three dozen BDs such as *American Picture Books, Texas Writers of Today,* and *Who's Who of Boys' Writers and Illustrators.*

Two other useful Gale Research BMIs are:

8. *An Analytical Bibliography of Universal Collected Biography.* 1980, reprint of the 1934 edition.

Indexes 56,000 biographies in over 3,000 books published before 1933—books like *Christian Heroes in the Army and Navy* by Charles Rogers (Low, 1867), *Mediaeval Preachers* by J. H. Neale (Mozley, 1873) and *Naval Heroes of Holland* by James Mets (1902).

9. *In Black and White: a Guide to Magazine Articles, Newspaper Articles and Books Concerning More than 15,000 Black Individuals and Groups.* 3d ed. 1980.

Some of the books indexed include *Negro Cowboys* by Philip Durham (Dodd Mead, 1965) and *Afro-American Artists* by Theresa Cederholm (Boston Public Library Trustees, 1973). Some of the magazines indexed are *Ebony, People, Black Sports, Sepia,* and *Jet.* Some newspapers included are the *Chicago Tribune,* the *Detroit Free Press,* the *San Francisco Examiner,* and the *Washington Post.*

The following BMIs are issued by various publishers.

10. *Index to Artistic Biography* compiled by Patricia Havlice. Scarecrow Press. 1973. Supplement, 1981.

Interfiles entries from about 135 books and BDs such as *American Folk Painters, Dictionary of British Bird Painters,* and *Women Artists: 1550-1950.*

11. *Index to Literary Biography* compiled by Patricia Havlice. 2 vols. Scarecrow Press. 1975. Suppl., 2 vols., 1983.

Interfiles entries from about 100 books and directories such as *American Writers in Paris, 1920-1939; Puerto Rican Authors,* and *Who's Who in Spy Fiction.*

12. *Marquis Who's Who Publications: Index to All Books.* Marquis Who's Who, Inc. 1974-date.

Interfiles the names from approximately fifteen Marquis Who's Who publications for the year. Titles covered include *Who's Who in America, Who's Who in the East, Who's Who in Government,* and *Who's Who in Religion.*

13. *Motion Picture Performers (MPP)* by Mel Schuster. Scarecrow Press. 1973. Supplement. 1976.

Cites articles in more than 250 magazines and selected books published between 1900 and 1974. (Newspapers are irregularly covered.) Some of the books indexed are *The Bad Guys* and *Who Is That?* Some magazines *MPP* indexes are *Coronet*, *Photoplay*, *Newsweek*, *Plays and Players*, *Seventeen*, *Time*, and *Vogue*.

Check your library for these BMIs, new revisions, and new titles that may come out.

IN-DEPTH BIOGRAPHICAL RESEARCH

What if entries in who's who books aren't enough? If you want everything you can find on someone, you must take a systematic approach so you can touch all bases.

Writings by the person

Has your subject written any books or articles? The following sources will tell you.

1. *National Union Catalog*. Library of Congress

2. *Books in Print*, author volume. 1948-date.

3. *Cumulative Book Index: a World List of Books in the English Language*. 1898-date.

4. *Book Reviews*. (See chapter 9.)

5. *Periodical Indexes*. (See chapter 7.)

First check your local library's catalog to see if the library owns anything by your subject.

Next, you'll want to see what else he or she has written that your library may not own. Several sources will tell you. One is the Library of Congress's published card catalog, the *National Union Catalog (NUC)*. It consists of more than 1,000 volumes arranged by author.

NUC is duplicated by *Cumulative Book Index (CBI)*, listing English-language books published worldwide, and the author volumes of *Books in Print (BIP)*. If you have access to *NUC*, skip *BIP* and *CBI*.

If your subject is famous, watch for a published bibliography on her or him in the tools above. It can reduce your research time considerably.

In the case of John Ehrlichman, the sources above show his published books. No bibliography of his work appears in print at this time.

Before you borrow the book or books written by your subject, you may want to check book reviews. They do more than summarize the books; they reflect public reaction to them.

Has your subject written any articles? By checking periodical indexes, you may find anything from the author's poetry to opinion pieces, autobiographical articles, or interviews.

Writings about the person

Some of the steps described earlier will identify writings about the person as well as by him. Consider the sources, however, in sorting the subjective from the objective.

If you don't find a bibliography on your subject through the previous steps, continue searching through the following sources:

1. *Biography Index*. 1946-date.

2. *Biographical Books, 1876-1949 and 1950-80*. 2 vols. R. R. Bowker Co.

3. *Subject Guide to Books in Print*. 1957-date.

4. *Library of Congress Dictionary Catalog: Subjects*. 1950-date.

Has your subject been the topic of magazine articles? (Newspapers are covered on page 92.)

Biography Index pulls biographical articles from many other indexes you would ordinarily not think to check. You may want to use others listed in chapter 7 which were published before *Biography Index* started in 1946. Note, too, that *Reader's Guide to Periodical Literature* first came out in 1905. If your subject dates to any time since then, check the appropriate years of the index.

Dozens of articles about John Ehrlichman appear in *Reader's Guide to Periodical Literature* in the 1970s. *Public Affairs Information Service Bulletin* for that period includes articles about him in some publications *RG* does not cover, such as *Congressional Quarterly Weekly Report* and *Weekly Compilation of Presidential Documents*.

The fastest way to identify biographies and autobiographies is to use *Biographical Books, 1876-1980*, a two-volume compilation of American books published about people in all fields. Use this tool before you try recent and back copies of *Subject Guide to Books in Print* and the *Library of Congress Dictionary Catalog: Subjects*, since they all overlap.

In this search, nothing appears in *Biographical Books* about Ehrlichman.

Articles and books may be useful in ways you don't anticipate. They sometimes list other readings in their bibliographies and provide clues to the location of original material in special library collections.

Local or regional sources

Everyone came from somewhere. Check issues of your subject's hometown newspaper through its index. You may have to do this by writing to the library in that community.

If the person was important in past city history, you might start first with the local historical society or library. It may own files that include old newspaper clippings (to save you a trip through indexes), family papers, and correspondence. Many libraries start files on natives of their city who have achieved widespread fame somewhere else. Consequently, information about a person may exist in more than one locality.

Depending on the kind of people research you're doing, you might have to approach it by subject. One researcher, with evidence that his great-grandfather worked on the construction of the Erie Canal, checked the Buffalo and Erie County Historical Society in New York for information about workers on the project. Lee Ash's *Subject Collections* referred him to this library when he checked the heading ERIE CANAL.

People in the news

If the person you're researching is newsworthy, large newspapers may carry relevant articles or obituaries. Several sources can lead you to them.

- Newspaper indexes.

- *NewsBank*.

- *Obituary Index to the New York Times*. 2 vols. 1858-1978. New York Times Co.

- *Obituaries from the [London] Times*. 3 vols. 1951-75. Newspaper Archive Developments, Ltd.

As already suggested, you can check newspaper indexes in different communities by mail. If your subject is prominent enough to appear in major newspapers like the *Washington Post*, check the related indexes in a large library.

Before checking *The New York Times*, always use the *Personal Name Index to the New York Times*. It makes names easier to find, since many get lost under other headings. People are often mentioned in scattered issues. Without the name index, it's hard to find all the issues their names appear in without a time-consuming search through many individual volumes.

Check the entry you find in the name index against the *New York Times Index* to get a summary of the article. If you decide that you want to read the article in full, you can read it on microfilm.

Use *NewsBank* to check a variety of newspapers around the country except *The New York Times*. (*NewsBank* is described in chapter 10.)

The books of obituaries above consolidate lengthy obituaries that ran in *The New York Times* and the *[London] Times*.

A person's affiliations

Is or was your subject a member of a prestigious club, a trade union, a corporation or other organization? Did the person found a college or hospital? Was a building named for your subject? Contact the library or public-relations offices of such organizations. They may have files of information that are not duplicated anywhere else.

If your search is derailed, contact an organization that may know about your subject, however remotely. People often ask me to find information about artists who use their first names only. In these cases, art galleries come to the rescue in providing last names.

Personal interviews

You may already have collected grudges, biases, and other shaded viewpoints about your subject from printed sources. Now it's time to get them directly from people.

Getting and conducting interviews is an art. The right way elicits rich information; the wrong way blocks answers.

Two books that will introduce you to the art of asking the right questoins are *How to Talk with Practically Anybody about Practically Anything* by Barbara Walters (Doubleday, 1983) and *The Craft of Interviewing* by John Brady (Random House, 1977). Both are filled with anecdotes and real-life experiences not only about well-known people but also about categories of people: The Bore, the handicapped, and the newly bereaved, to name some.

Another book, *Conversationally Speaking*, by Alan Garner (McGraw-Hill, 1981), can help you if you're shy. Garner's practical tips will teach you how to start and maintain a conversation in almost any situation.

Unpublished material

At some point, you may want to bypass published material and go right to such original writings as diaries, notebooks, correspondence, and other personal papers. These materials are called *primary sources*.

Primary sources are often donated to libraries, archives, and historical societies. Some are still in private hands. How can you find them?

You may be tipped off to private caches at any stage of your research. Clues to their location often pop up in footnotes or articles. You can also do as many researchers do—place ads in literary or book-review magazines such as the *New York Times Book Review* to draw out privately held material.

Many public collections of personal papers are recorded in certain reference books. Check chapter 15 for more on locating personal papers in public collections.

Before you give up on the idea of a biography, review the approaches outlined in this chapter. Rich veins of information may be available for mining—by you.

13
ADDRESSES AND
PHONE NUMBERS

How can you locate Steven Spielberg to discuss your screenplay? Or the president of an herbal tea company for an article you're writing?

People and organizations aren't always easy to find. They often move, change their names, or die. Sometimes they don't want to be found. You *can* approach address research just as systematically as you approach your other research.

You've already been introduced to many reference books that give addresses. Most current biographical dictionaries discussed in the previous chapter, for example, include them. The list below suggests other tools to try.

TELEPHONE BOOKS

Large libraries carry a selection of telephone books from around the nation. If you call, a librarian can often check one for you.

Many libraries are replacing their paper phone books with *Phonefiche*, a collection of more than 1,400 telephone directories on microfiche, giving you access to more phone numbers than ever before.

Let's look at ways you can use phone books, some of which you may be unaware of.

Perhaps you're looking for a social service agency in a city but you don't know the agency's name. In some cases, you'll find it by checking a keyword in the White Pages. For example, if you check the words *fire* or *police*, you might find the listing for your city fire and police stations. Try the same for hotlines and associations. Check *drug* and you might find a drug counseling center. Under the word *children* in the San Diego White Pages, I found listings for the Children's Information Network and Children's Hospital. In some cities you can send your consumer complaint to any of the agencies listed under *consumer complaint*.

Are you looking for a business? Is it possible that it's part of a chain? If so, its Yellow or White Page listing may include a toll-free number for the national headquarters in another city.

The telephone books for Manhattan and Washington, D.C., are valuable as ordinary reference books. Librarians have a theory: If you can't find an address quickly, check these phone books. I've found many addresses of national associations, companies, and government agencies and subagencies by name or keyword in these White Pages.

The Yellow Pages for Manhattan and Washington, D.C., are also invaluable. Someone once asked me to find a special kind of imported light bulb. After checking manufacturers directories and finding nothing, I tried the Manhattan Yellow Pages, where I found a company ad mentioning the very product I was looking for.

THE *ZIP CODE DIRECTORY*

On the first page of each city's entry in the *ZIP Code Directory (ZCD)* you'll find the street addresses of major hotels, motels, apartment buildings, hospitals, office buildings, colleges, and government buildings. Large libraries usually have a copy of the *ZCD*. Pilot Books also sells a pocket edition for about four dollars.

OTHER DIRECTORIES

Are you looking for a bird club? How about a convention center, a toy manufacturer, a radio or TV station, a nuclear-power plant, a foundation, a medical specialist, a pension fund, a kiddie park, or companies in the solar energy field? You'll find them listed in directories.

Libraries keep current directories in their reference departments. The *Directory of Directories (DOD)* (Information Research Enterprises, 1980-date) lists more than 5,000 of them. *DOD* will also help you identify the directories you need for your market research, such as *Writer's Market* and *News Bureaus in the U.S.*

If you want to get a directory your library doesn't own, borrow it through interlibrary loan. Some library somewhere will have that specialized directory you want and may lend you last year's copy.

The following list includes eleven directories for writers found through *DOD:*

1. *Ayer Directory of Publications.* Ayer Press. 1880-date. Annual.

Lists 21,000 newspapers and magazines published in the United States and Canada. Special appendixes list publications by category (foreign language, college, labor, etc.) and newspapers by circulation with the name of the editor of each section (food, travel, etc.).

2. *Directory of Small Magazine Press Editors and Publishers.* Dustbooks. 1970-date. Annual.

Covers 3,500 small publishers and literary magazines with publication and submission requirements.

3. *Fiction Writer's Market.* Writer's Digest Books. 1981-date. Annual.

Lists over 1,200 magazines, book publishers, and small presses that buy short stories, poetry, and novels for adult and youth markets. Includes articles offering instruction and writing tips.

4. *How to Enter and Win Fiction Writing Contests* by Alan Gadney. Facts on File, Inc. 1981.
Lists some 500 contest sources with rules and qualifications for entering them.

5. *How to Enter and Win Nonfiction and Journalism Contests* by Alan Gadney. Facts on File, Inc. 1981.
Some 400 contest sources are listed here, with rules and qualifications.

6. *International Directory of Little Magazines and Small Presses.* Dustbooks. 1965-date. Annual.
A guide to about 3,500 poetry and essay markets that offer little or no pay. Includes small publishers, many of which are not in other guides.

7. *Literary Market Place (LMP).* R. R. Bowker Co. 1940-date. Annual.
LMP lists varied services in publishing—over 1,430 book publishers and organizations that issue three or more books annually; book printers; binders; syndicates; periodicals; radio and TV stations that do book reviews: agents; literary organizations; and more.

8. *Publisher's Trade List Annual (PTLA).* 5 vols. R. R. Bowker Co. 1873-date. Annual.
PTLA is a collection of some 1,800 publishers' backlist catalogs. (Not every press is included.) This is a useful aid in selecting a publisher.

9. *Working Press of the Nation.* 5 vols. National Research Bureau. 1947-date. Annual.
Lists syndicates, daily and weekly newspapers, radio and TV stations, magazines and house organs, and the names of free-lance feature writers and photographers.

10. *Writers and Artist's Yearbook.* A & C Black Publishers, Ltd. 1906-date. Annual.
Listings of book publishers, book clubs, magazines, syndicates, poetry markets, broadcasters, photography libraries, etc., in England, Australia, Canada, India, Ireland, and New Zealand that buy free-lance material or offer services to free-lancers. Includes information on selling screenplays and getting an agent in Britain.

11. *Writer's Market (WM).* Writer's Digest Books. 1930-date. Annual.
WM lists more than 700 publishers and 4,000 magazines, syndicates, agents, script buyers, gag and filler markets, and greeting card publishers with purchasing requirements and general pay rates.
Besides these eleven, many other directories may be useful. The *Directory of Directories*, for example, lists the following:

- *Hang Glider Directory*
- *Tennessee Directory of Manufacturers*
- *American Labor Sourcebook*
- *Woodall's Campground Directory*
- *Polk's World Bank Directory*
- *Directory of Conventions*

WHEN AN ADDRESS ELUDES YOU

Having tried everything you can think of, you still may not find an address you need. Consider some of the following tips to get yourself back on track.

The multistep approach

You won't find all addresses using the direct approach. For example, you may have to read a magazine or newspaper article for a clue to someone's home base. A sidebar accompanying a magazine article on collecting baseball cards may mention the national association of baseball card collectors you couldn't find anywhere else.

At times, you'll have to use a creative or devious approach. For example, you may have to send a letter in care of a publisher, bank, college, club, or other organization with whom your subject is affiliated, asking to have it forwarded. Or, you may prefer to check European companies in American directories, since many have branches here.

Beware of old directories

If you're using an old directory, check an address you find there against the most recent source. Sending letters to the wrong address can delay replies beyond your deadline.

Check for unusual directory arrangements

Remember to check the directory's plan. Flip through the pages and skim the table of contents and the index. Is it arranged alphabetically, geographically, by subject? Does it include separate appendixes or addendums for late entries?

Not all phone books that cover several communities in a county, for example, interfile the names from each community into one alphabet. Names are sometimes separated into different community lists, making it easy to miss someone who is really there.

Many other research traps previously discussed may come into play here. Take filing order, for example. Many San Diegans can't find Rich Wise's public-relations firm in the local phone book because the firm is listed under *Wise Communications* (after *Wise, Charles,* rather than *Wise, Rich, Communications.*

Categorize

People and groups without phones are not in the phone book. Even those with a phone can choose to omit their address from the telephone directory. In such cases, categorize your search and try a different directory instead. For example, the California Genealogical Society lists no street address in the San Francisco phone book, but does appear in the *Directory of Historical Societies and Agencies in the United States and Canada*.

Use the specific approach

Whenever possible, select a directory offering a specific rather than a general focus. If the International Yellow Pages is the same size as the San Diego Yellow Pages, how comprehensive can it be?

Specific directories—subject, product, or regional—are usually more complete than general or all-encompassing directories. Far more Iowa manufacturers appear in *Directory of Iowa Manufacturers* than in the *Thomas Register of American Manufacturers*.

Use more than one directory

Since no reference book includes everyone or everything, check every directory you find on your topic. Don't abandon your search after trying just one. We've already seen that the *Thomas Register of American Manufacturers* doesn't include every manufacturer in the country. (The Los Angeles Yellow Pages lists more clothing manufacturers in that city than the *Thomas Register* lists for the entire state of California.)

Maybe a business consists of one person operating from a home address or post office box number; some groups survive only a short time and fade out before appearing in directories. An individual or group may just have achieved fame or begun operating. In that case, you might be checking too soon.

Many directories overlook people or groups because there's no systematic or reliable way for a compiler to find them. Sometimes a person or organization in a related business or field can come to the rescue.

OLD ADDRESSES IN HISTORICAL RESEARCH

Maybe you want to know where someone or something used to be.

Many annual directories have been around for decades. An old edition allows you to reconstruct history. The 1907 edition of *Ayer Directory of Publications* will tell you the name of the major newspaper in Newark, New Jersey, at that time; *Patterson's American Education*, 1925 edition, will name all high schools in New Orleans in 1925; the 1890 issue of the *Hotel & Motel Redbook* (then called *The United States Official Hotel Directory*), will identify hotels in Miami Beach that year.

To determine the starting publication date of any directory or magazine, check *Union List of Serials* and its recent volumes, *New Serial Titles*. If you follow these rules diligently, you should be able to find almost every address you need.

14
STATISTICS

Sooner or later in your writing you'll need to quote a statistic. Whether those numbers document, support, or dramatize a statement, statistics lend authority. First, however, you must find them.

WHERE DO STATISTICS COME FROM?

Most statistics emanate from academic, industry, private, or government research.

Academic or scholarly research is concentrated in the sciences and the humanities. Scholarly research may study, for example, the phenomenon of blaming the victim or the cure rate for various diseases in the past twenty years. Whatever the topic of the study, statistics result.

Research sponsored by corporations, organizations, or industry groups usually generates hard data: the number of nursing homes in Maine, the growth of satellite TV sales in the past decade. The data may be collected to provide public information about that industry or to enhance its image.

Uncle Sam thrives on statistics. Without them, the government could not apportion funds or determine the number of representatives per state. In fulfilling their duties, the varied agencies, departments, and bureaus of the government issue countless statistics.

State and county governments also issue statistics, whether you're looking for data on the state's foster-home care or airport funding.

Locally, you may want to determine the number of billboards in the city, alcohol use among certain groups of citizens, or the impact of a federal tax reduction on local services. Whatever the topic of the study, statistics will be included.

STATISTICAL INDEXES

Just as the hundreds of biographical dictionaries are listed in master indexes, so are hundreds of statistical sources.

Three major indexes to statistics are published by Congressional Information Service, Inc. (CIS) in Washington, D.C. Together, they locate thousands of charts and tables contained within directories, annual reports, and magazine articles.

1. *American Statistics Index (ASI)*. 1974-date.

ASI covers statistics in publications issued by state and federal governmental agencies such as the National Aeronautics and Space Administration (NASA), Central Intelligence Agency (CIA), the Veterans Administration (VA), and others mentioned in chapter 11.

2. *Index to International Statistics (IIS)*. 1983-date.

IIS indexes statistics that appear in the publications of more than three dozen United Nations agencies and commissions and dozens of other international, intergovernmental organizations, such as the Organization of Petroleum Exporting Countries (OPEC), the United Nations Educational, Scientific, and Cultural Organization (UNESCO), the World Bank Group, and the Economic Commission for Latin America.

3. *Statistical Reference Index (SRI)*. 1980-date.

SRI locates statistics in publications issued by commercial publishers (*Publishers Weekly*), associations (*Barber Schools, Barber Students, and Barber Statistics*, issued by the National Association of Barber Schools); business or commercial organizations (*Discount Store News*, issued by Lebhar-Friedman), university research centers (*Indiana Business Review*, issued by Indiana University School of Business), and some state agencies (*State of Oklahoma Uniform Crime Report*, issued by the Oklahoma Bureau of Investigation).

Although these indexes include different publications, the subjects they cover are similar. For example, most of the following subjects appear in all three indexes.

ENDANGERED SPECIES	FOSTER HOME CARE
ENERGY CONSERVATION	FRAUD
FAMILY ABANDONMENT	GAMBLING
FEDERAL AID TO HOUSING	HOURS OF LABOR
FETAL DEATHS	IMMIGRATION

The indexes include more than recent statistics. For example, even though they started publication in 1974, 1983, and 1980, respectively, each contains charts for periods prior to those dates.

How to use the CIS statistical indexes

Each index comes out monthly and cumulates into a single volume at the end of the year. To find a statistic, check the index volume by subject. This is what an entry from the 1984 *SRI* index looks like:

FETAL DEATHS
    Spermicide users possibility of bearing female infant and losing fetus, 1973-76 survey, article. A5160-1.501

Copy the number next to the citation (A5160-1.501) and look it up in the abstract volume. The information there includes a summary of the chart's contents and the title of the publication in which it originally ran:

A5160-1 *Family Planning Perspectives.* Bimonthly.
A5160-1.501: Sept./Oct. 1983 (Vol. 15, No. 5)
Contraceptive continuation among adolescents attending family planning clinics.

(p. 211-217) by Frank F. Furstenberg, Jr. et al. Article evaluating interview methods used to assess contraceptive practices among teenagers. Data are from a study of 445 female adolescents using 9 federally funded family planning clinics in Philadelphia, Pa., Jan. 1980-Sept. 1981.

The rest of the annotation describes the kinds of statistics and tables the article includes.

To see the article in full, first find out whether your library owns the publication it appears in. If not, ask if the library owns the microform sets of documents that come with the indexes. Your last alternative would be to try interlibrary loan.

Other statistical indexes

What if none of the Congressional Information Service indexes is available in your area or they don't cover the time period you need? Smaller indexes to statistics are available, and they cover many of the same directories as the CIS indexes.

1. *Encyclopedia of Business Information Sources (EBIS)* Gale Research Co. Issued every three to five years.

EBIS is an excellent guide that identifies a variety of reference books—dictionaries, handbooks, statistics sources, etc. It also includes a list of statistical publications, many of them covered by the CIS statistics indexes.

Entries are arranged by subject, followed by categories—dictionaries, handbooks, statistics sources—and the titles of recommended books.

Samples of some categories and statistical publications listed are as follows:

COURTS
STATISTICS SOURCES
Juvenile Court Statistics. Issued annually by the Social
Rehabilitation Service of the DHEW.
CREDIT
STATISTICS SOURCES
Federal Reserve Bulletin. Issued monthly by the Government
Printing Office.
Credit and Capital Markets. Issued annually by Bankers Trust Co.
CRIME AND CRIMINALS
STATISTICS SOURCES

Crime in the United States. Issued annually by the FBI.
Prisoners in State and Federal Institutions. Issued annually by the
Department of Justice.

2. *Statistics Sources (SS),* edited by Paul Wasserman. Gale Research Co.
Issued every five to seven years.

SS covers over 150 government and commercially published statistics
directories. Most are issued annually or biannually.

The topics covered are similar to those in other statistics indexes:
CHILE—BEER PRODUCTION; CHILE—BIRTH RATE; CIGARETTES—
PRICES; CIRRHOSIS OF LIVER—DEATHS: DOMINICAN REPUBLIC—DE-
FENSE EXPENDITURES, etc. Entries include the publication in which the
chart or table appears.

STATISTICAL YEARBOOKS

The statistics indexes already described refer to many major statistical
yearbooks, including the *United Nations Statistical Yearbook* and the *Statistical Abstracts of the United States.* If no indexes to statistics are handy, you
can still use the statistical yearbooks individually. Here are some, together with samples of data they cover.

Statistical yearbooks covering several countries

Some yearbooks report statistics for more than 100 countries. These
include the annual *UNESCO Statistical Yearbook* (1963-date) and the annual *United Nations Statistical Yearbook* (1948-date).

The *UNESCO Statistical Yearbook* focuses on statistics in the arts and
culture for more than 125 countries. It covers such topics as school enroll-
ments in various countries, percentages of repeaters by grade, numbers
of college graduates by major, numbers of children's book titles and copies published, radios in use, etc.

The *United Nations Statistical Yearbook* covers statistics in general subjects—arts, sciences, economics, etc. It covers such data as government
receipts and public debt, balance of payments, output and employment
in manufacturing, wholesale and retail trade, numbers of motor vehicles
in use, and unemployment rates.

Statistical yearbooks covering individual countries

Statistical yearbooks for individual countries list categories similar to
those covered by groups of countries and in addition, specific data. For
example, *Year Book—Australia* breaks figures down by region of the country, while figures reported in the UN and UNESCO yearbooks cover Australia as a whole.

Look for the statistical yearbooks of major countries through a library's catalog under the name of the country followed by the term STA-
TISTICS. You can also identify them through one of Joan Harvey's bibliographies: *Statistics/Europe; Statistics/Asia and Australasia; Statistics/Africa;*

and *Statistics/America (North, Central & South)*.

Post-1970 statistical yearbooks for approximately seventy-five Third World countries from Fiji to Botswana are covered in a microfiche collection called *Current National Statistical Compendium*.

Statistical yearbooks for each state

Most of the charts in the *Statistical Abstract of the United States*, issued annually by the U. S. Department of Commerce (1878-date) report figures for the nation as a whole. Some of its charts list such data as franchised new-car dealerships, 1970-83; immigrants admitted by classes, 1930-81; preprimary-school enrollment, 1968-83; crime rates, 1980-83 (by state and type of crime); attendance at selected spectator sports, 1970-83; and mortgage debt outstanding and delinquent, 1970-84 (by type of mortgage).

Some states issue their own statistics directories, such as *Florida Statistical Abstract* and *Statistical Abstract of Louisiana*. Much of the information breaks down by county. Data covered in state statistical abstracts include, for example, mode of transportation used by workers aged sixteen and over; miles of road under state, local, and federal control; revenue collected from car tags; operations at individual airports within the state; and a breakdown of state phone companies.

Historical statistics

Some yearbooks cover statistics over several centuries. These can help you make interesting comparisons.

1. *European Historical Statistics, 1750-1975*. 2d ed. Facts on File 1980.

This useful yearbook covers dozens of subjects over a 225-year period, such as the area of vineyards and wine output in Italy from 1861 to date, government revenue and main tax yields in Germany from 1900 to date, mail volume in France from 1830 to date, and the number of motor vehicles in use in Denmark from 1910 to date.

2. *Historical Abstracts of the U. S.: Colonial Times to 1970*. U. S. Department of Commerce 1975.

This yearbook gives similar statistics for the United States. It provides such information as the number of households with radio sets, 1922-70; radio and TV advertising expenditures, 1935-70; recorded mergers in manufacturing and mining, 1895-1970; the number of firms in operation by major industry group, 1929-63; money-market rates, 1890-1970; bond and stock yields, 1857-1970; electoral votes cast for president by state and political party, 1804-1968; the cost of presidential general elections, 1860-1968; and estimates of the total costs of U. S. wars.

UNINDEXED STATISTICS

Not all statistics are neatly arranged in charts and tables in statistical handbooks. In many cases, the figures are buried within the text of a book or dissertation, or an article not covered by a statistical index.

A variety of reference books, such as almanacs, also include statistics. Almanacs reprint charts from other sources. For example, a chart in the 1984 *World Almanac* showing the fuel economy in miles per gallon of 1984 autos comes from the U.S. Environmental Protection Agency. A chart showing the world daily dietary energy supply in relation to requirements comes from the UN Food and Agriculture Organization.

Charts in the *Standard Education Almanac* offer figures on employment trends and dropout rates in adult education, trends in college enrollment for a ten-year period, and the number of full-time teachers in public schools by age.

Yearbooks include varied statistics, too. The *Yearbook of American and Canadian Churches*, for example, includes such data as total membership, church attendance, finances, number of churches, clergy, and Sunday schools by denomination.

Dissertations are still another source of unindexed statistics. Though many dissertations are mentioned in such periodical indexes as *Psychological Abstracts*, they're also listed in an index of their own—*Dissertation Abstracts International (DAI)* (University Microfilms International).

DAI is an annual list of dissertations written at approximately 500 participating American and foreign colleges and universities from 1861 to the present. To find a dissertation by subject, check the keyword index entitled *Comprehensive Dissertation Index, 1861-1972* and annual updates. *DAI* comes both in a hardcopy set and in microform.

Look for a dissertation by keyword. The following is a sample entry from *DAI* (1984):

> STRESS·
> Institutional correlates of stress/burnout as perceived by early childhood teachers.—Weekes, Yvonne Nona (Ed. D. 1982 Columbia University Teachers College) 151 p. 43/10A p. 3262 DEP 83-04053

Every major word in a dissertation title is indexed.

The abstract of this dissertation appears on page 3262 in volume 43, number 10 of the set marked A, which covers humanities and social science dissertations. (Set B covers science and engineering dissertations.) DEP 83-04053 is the order number to use if you want to buy your own copy of the dissertation.

Libraries own many dissertations reprinted by University Microfilms, so you may find the one you want in a large library. If the library you use doesn't own it, borrow it on interlibrary loan.

Every number you use in your writing must come from a substantiated source. Whether that source is a government report, a magazine article, or a Ph. D. dissertation, the indexes in this chapter should help you find what you need.

15
ORIGINAL RESEARCH

There are three major ways to write a nonfiction book. You can write it from printed resources, base it on experience—your own or someone else's—or you can use original material and draw your own conclusions. In many cases, a combination of these approaches works best.

Original materials are largely unpublished. They may be correspondence, reports, bank books, diaries, mortgage papers, even old resumes. Papers we sign in the course of living, such as marriage certificates, property records, baptismal records, and military enlistment papers are also original materials.

Facts from such materials as they filter through the work of different writers become distorted, exaggerated, and changed. A house located on Fir St. may, over the years, accidentally change to First St. By using original documents, you can reconstruct and often correct errors that have been misinterpreted in transmission.

WHERE IS ORIGINAL MATERIAL?

Original, unpublished material is everywhere. Any individual, public agency, association, church, or business that keeps records about its activities is a potential source of original material. It may be stored with the group that originated it or kept by libraries, museums, historical societies, or any of the other information providers mentioned in chapter 1.

Public records are varied—vital (birth, death, marriage) records, church or synagogue records, probate, land, naturalization, census, military, educational, and miscellaneous federal records such as pension records, court-martial papers, and passport applications. These are filed with public agencies in a city or county. When they accumulate into larger collections, they are usually transferred to a centralized agency in the state capital. Federal records, such as military records, are eventually sent to the National Archives.

Genealogy books are useful for detailed descriptions and locations of public records by state. Three helpful books to check are *Genealogical Research: Methods and Resources,* edited by Milton Rubincam; *The Researcher's Guide to American Genealogy* by Val D. Greenwood; and *How to Find Your Family Roots* by Timothy Beard.

ORIGINAL MATERIAL IN MICROFORM

Along with books, newspapers, and magazines, micropublishers are filming the papers of organizations and well-known individuals as well as special subject collections of different libraries. Now you have access to correspondence, notebooks, pamphlets, and other ephemeral and unpublished material that formerly existed in only one location.

The list below reflects a small but varied selection of the many original materials in microform. Most come with printed guides. You can find many others by checking micropublishers' catalogs in large libraries.

Special collections

1. *The FBI Files on the Assassination of President Kennedy.* Contains letters, FBI memos, files on Lee Harvey Oswald, and Warren Commission files.

2. *Books about North American Indians on Microfilm.* Consists of more than 660 books on microfilm.

Organization papers

Organization papers include minutes, newspaper clippings, reports, and correspondence. Some of the correspondence is lengthy and spans many years, even decades. You may find letters penned by people whose names are now well known in history. They may be useful if you're writing a biography of someone who was connected with a well-known organization.

Organization papers are on file with the national headquarters or in a microform collection in a library. Sample collections in microform are:

1. *Southern Tenant Farmers Union Papers, 1934-70.* This was a group of Southern sharecroppers involved in the civil rights movement. The original papers are in the University of North Carolina Library in Chapel Hill.

2. *American Labor Unions' Constitutions and Proceedings 1836-1980.* These papers were assembled from labor union repositories and about a dozen libraries.

Also check Lee Ash's *Subject Collections* to locate original organization papers in libraries. Some groups listed, for example, are the National Theatre Conference (papers in the Indiana University at Bloomington), the National Urban League and the National Woman's Party (papers in the Library of Congress).

Personal papers

By examining the personal papers of individuals who influenced history, we have a better undertanding of those events as well as the individuals themselves. A sample collection:

■*Horatio Gates Papers, 1726-1828.*
Gates was a Revolutionary War hero. His papers consist of such items as orderly books and correspondence with such major figures as Thomas Jefferson and Benedict Arnold. Most of the material in the collection came from the New York Historical Society, with contributions from more than seventy other libraries.

Also microfilmed are the papers of other prominent political and historical figures such as Jimmy Carter, George Washington Carver, Aaron Burr, and John L. Lewis.

HOW TO IDENTIFY
THE ORIGINAL MATERIAL YOU'LL NEED

Several reference books may be useful in helping you locate collections of original materials.

1. *The National Union Catalog of Manuscript Collections (NUCMC).* Library of Congress. 1959-date. Annual.
Contents. NUCMC lists minutes, scrapbooks, correspondence, record books, photos, newsletters, clippings, etc. of scientists, local politicians and business owners, ordinary citizens, clergy, teachers, soldiers, authors, and others, representing all walks of life as well as organizations, companies, chambers of commerce, orphanages, businesses, and other groups. The directory is not comprehensive.
Arrangement. Check the subject index in each volume or the cumulative indexes covering several years by individual name or organization or by subject.

2. *Subject Collections: A Guide to Special Book Collections and Subject Emphases as Reported by Universities, Colleges, Public and Special Libraries and Museums in the U.S. and Canada (SC)* by Lee Ash. R. R. Bowker Co. Published every five to seven years.
Contents. SC describes major special collections. If a printed catalog was issued that describes the collection in greater detail, its title will appear at the bottom of the entry. Many libraries own these printed catalogs.
Arrangement. Entries are alphabetical by subject—NATIONAL VOLLEYBALL ASSOCIATION, NATURALISTS, NAUTICAL CHARTS, NAVAJO INDIANS, NAVAL HISTORY, etc.

3. *Women's History Sources: A Guide to Archives and Manuscript Collections in the U.S. (WHS).* 2 vols. R. R. Bowker Co. 1979.
Contents. The compilers of this large resource have analyzed hundreds of published and unpublished guides to archives to create a single

index of women's history sources. *WHS* also includes references to men, societies, book titles, organizations, newspapers, churches, etc. connected with women's studies.

Arrangement. A typical entry looks like this:

    IOWA
        IOWA CITY
            4,936. Mather, Samuel.
                Papers. 1869-1951. 1 ft.
                Open. Inventory.
                State Historical Society.

                Photo albums and clippings of a West Liberty, IA, Quaker
                family that worked in dry goods and farming. Includes photos
                depicting the college days, home, relatives, and marriage of
                Samuel Mather's daughter, Rachel Mather, 1890-1919.

Uses *WHS's* geographical index to identify the collections in libraries and archives in your area.

You can find other directories of archives by checking *Subject Guide to Books in Print* or the library's catalog under the headings ARCHIVES and MANUSCRIPTS. Your search will identify such directories as the *Guide to Manuscripts Relating to the American Indian in the Library of the American Philosophical Society*.

USING SECONDARY MATERIAL
IN ORIGINAL RESEARCH

Once a book or article is published, it becomes a secondary resource. As successive authors use it for their research (and other authors use *their* works), the chances of inaccuracy and misinterpretation multiply.

All material—published and unpublished—contains biases and errors. In annual directories, for example, it's normal to find many outdated addresses and phone numbers because publishers cannot confirm every single item for the new addition. In unpublished materials, people copy incorrectly and subjectively.

Nevertheless, many published (i.e. secondary) resources are useful, if not essential, to original research. An old city newspaper might help you document the date of a theater performance or a train wreck. An old almanac may cite the name of a college president in 1919. A reprint of a 1596 book on sixteenth-century religious beliefs (*The Historie of Heaven*) might offer different insights on the subject than one published more recently.

HOW TO SPOT INACCURACIES

If everything you read is subject to factual errors or biases, how can you interpret information correctly?

You must constantly compare the data you collect with an eye for mismatches. One source may place Ernest Hemingway in one location on a particular date; another source will say he was somewhere else. Only continued research can help you break the impasse.

To interpret material correctly, you may have to study the background of a period or event to understand the attitudes that prevailed at the time. What was the public mood in the United States during the McCarthy era? Why did hemlines go up in the 1960s? Without knowing the emotion that a person or event evoked in an era, we're prey to misinterpretations. We recognize gossip magazines and extremist literature today, but how do we judge and interpret those of the past? How will future writers judge those of our day?

Just how much fact checking and analysis must you do without impairing your progress? You can draw from a hazy recollection, or you can try to verify a point from several different sources. You can make something up, or you can call someone who should know. To be sure, it's not possible to check every single fact in your article or book, but you can expend reasonable effort to minimize the chance of error.

If your work is to be creditable, it must be based on sound research, not guesses or assumptions. Your conclusions require proof. Publishers have more than once recalled books whose facts were challenged.

Writing is a responsibility that carries some risk. The job is considerably easier when you make an honest effort to get the facts. Using original and old material will give you that chance.

16
QUOTATIONS

A vivid phrase or a quotation is like the proverbial picture—it's worth ten thousand words. There are times when you'll want to use quotations in your writing.

A quotation can be many things: a line from a song, nursery rhyme, poem, speech, novel, or newspaper, or magazine article. It can be a title of a book, play, or song; a speech, slogan, pun, or someone's last words. A quotation is anything that has been spoken, written, or even sung, and above all, it's memorable or catchy.

> At three o'clock Thursday afternoon, Theodore Roosevelt will walk on the waters of Lake Michigan.
>
> —Anon.
>
> Handbill distributed at the Republican convention
> June, 1912, Chicago.

There are several approaches to finding a quotation. You may want to determine who said it or how it originated. Or, having just a few keywords, you may want to get the correct wording. The last approach is to look for a quotation by subject.

Finding quotations is like other forms of research—there's a pattern to follow. At times, however, you won't find the quotation you're after. The tips below will help make your search easier and also explain why you sometimes can't find a quotation you know everyone has heard.

TEN TIPS

1. General quotation books vary greatly. Some focus on classical expressions, others emphasize modern sayings. Some are subject oriented and quote expressions from motion pictures or science, for example; some contain a little of everything. Because of these wide differences, you'll usually have to check more than one quotation book in your search.

2. Seldom does one recall a quotation verbatim. A mistake in a single word may prevent you from finding it. Was it "My feet are heavy now ..." or "Thy feet are heavy now ..."? Be careful of misplaced or incorrect words.

3. Clues are vital. A title, author, subject, first line, a striking phrase,

where and when you heard it—anything is potentially helpful. Mention such clues when a librarian is helping you.

4. Start with the best-known and biggest quotation books (back editions as well as recent editions):
■ *Familiar Quotations* by John Bartlett. 15th ed. Little, Brown. 1980. 1,540 pages.

Bartlett's is arranged chronologically by the birth date of the person quoted—Thorstein Veblen, 1857-1929; Theodore Roosevelt, 1858-1919; Sir Arthur Conan Doyle, 1859-1930. In most cases, you'll start with the keyword index to see if it includes the quotations you're researching.

■ *Home Book of Quotations (HBQ)* by Burton Stevenson. 10th ed. Dodd, Mead. 1967. 2,816 pages.

Sources quoted are heavily classical and historical, such as Aristophanes, Swift, Edmund Burke, William Penn, Shakespeare, Lord Halifax.

HBQ is arranged alphabetically by subject: MEMORY, MERCY, MERIT, MERMAID, MERRIMENT, MIDNIGHT. It also includes keyword and author indexes. You'll likely start your search with the keyword index.

■ *Dictionary of Quotations (DQ)* by Bergan Evans. Delacorte Press. 1968. 2,029 pages.

DO contains a combination of popular contemporary and classical quotations. It's arranged alphabetically by subject and includes keyword and author indexes.

5. Search lesser-known quotation books. There are hundreds in print, and you may want to find something more relevant than the three mentioned above. See *Subject Guide to Books in Print* under the term QUOTATIONS for titles of others. For example, *Dictionary of Sexist Quotations* would be best to check for a sexist quotation; *Cree's Dictionary of Latin Quotations* probably includes more Latin sayings than *Bartlett's*.

6. If you have a reputed author or a first line or title of a poem or song, check a poetry index, the author's collected works, or a song index before trying a quotation book.

Check the library's catalog under the author's name to find his or her collected works. Some collected works include a keyword index to help you find a particular poem more quickly.

7. Shakespeare and the Bible are prolific sources of quotations, but general quotation books include only a small sampling of them. Instead, check concordances (word-by-word dictionaries) such as *Young's Analytical Concordance to the Bible* or *Bartlett's Complete Concordance to Shakespeare*.

8. Not all quotation books are kept in a library's reference department.

Large libraries keep some in the circulating stacks to be checked out.

9. If all else fails, ask a librarian. Since quotations questions are handled often, many libraries keep in-house files and other aids to make the job easier. The Los Angeles Public Library, for example, has created a joint card file index of all editions of *Bartlett's Familiar Quotations* published since 1855.

10. Remember, a less than 50 percent success rate in tracing quotations is normal. Quotation books say that their goal is to record memorable sayings, yet they confess that they cannot define what is memorable. Furthermore, not everything quotable has been written down.

You'll also find that some quotations are incorrectly attributed. "The only thing necessary for the triumph of evil is for good men to do nothing" is an aphorism reputedly but not proven to be Edmund Burke's. Other quotations such as "the whole nine yards" have more than one theory on their origins. Many quotations, such as "killing the messenger" have still not been traced.

HOW TO LOOK UP A QUOTATION

Most quotation books have keyword indexes that occupy up to half the book. If you want to verify a quotation's accuracy or its speaker, start with the index.

The next question is, which keyword in the quotation should you check? As a sample, let's use "A stitch in time saves nine."

The index in *Bartlett's Familiar Quotations* lists the saying under two keywords:

> Stitch in time saves nine
> Nine, stitch in time saves n.

There is nothing under SAVES and TIME.

The index in Stevenson's book lists the saying under one keyword only: STITCH.

The index in Evans's book doesn't include the saying at all.

As these examples show, it's best to check as many keywords in a quotation as possible.

A SELECTION OF QUOTATION BOOKS

Don't feel overwhelmed with the huge number of quotation books that exist. Remember, none is comprehensive, and many won't be pertinent to your needs. Sample quotations from a selection of books will give you some idea of the scope available.

■ *Macmillan Book of Business and Economic Quotes*, edited by Michael Jackman. Macmillan Publishing Co. 1984.

LEISURE
Few people do business well who do nothing else.

—Lord Chesterfield, 1749

■ *The Movie Quote Book* by Harry Haun. Lippincott & Crowell. 1980.
ELEPHANTS
One morning I shot an elephant in my pajamas. How he got into
my pajamas I'll never know.

—Groucho Marx giving an African lecture
in Victor Hierman's *Animal Crackers.*

■ *The Morrow Book of Quotations in American History* by Joseph Conlin.
William Morrow and Co. 1984
JAMES A. GARFIELD (1831-1881): Twentieth president.
My God! What is there in this place that a man should ever want
to get into it?

(On the flood of office seekers, June 1881).

A terse, well-placed quotation may be just what you need to express
your point precisely.

17
PICTURE RESEARCH

Visual material adds life to a printed page; you may want to consider using some. Certain topics—a space flight or gardening, for example—demand illustrations. Since reproductions of almost anything from dinosaurs to the latest fashions are collected by somebody somewhere, you should be able to get something appropriate for your project.

GETTING PICTURES

You can buy or lease photographs, get them free of charge, or take your own. You can also use old illustrations no longer restricted by copyright. Each path presents different problems, most of which concern your deadline and your budget.

Use pictures that ran in other publications

A simple way to get pictures is to note the photograph credits in other books and magazines (the Metropolitan Museum of Art, the Library of Congress, etc.) and contact these sources. Using photographs that have already been seen may not guarantee originality in your work, but getting them is often quick and inexpensive. Photocopy the picture from the publication in which you saw it (for identification), and request prints.

Check *Subject Guide to Books in Print* for books on any subject—astronomy, butterflies, plastic art, aircraft, etc.—that contain illustrations. (Entries should be marked 'illus,' though many books with illustrations are not.) If the book is not more than about twenty-five years old, it should credit its picture sources.

Start a search close to home

It's faster and easier to start any information hunt close to home. Where pictures are concerned, you'll want to see them before ordering prints. Local sources can provide more than you think.

Pictures from regional historical societies, for example, transcend geography. Old-time fashions, a horse and buggy, or a muddy street scene can exist anywhere. Historical societies may also lend daguerreotypes, posters, old greeting cards, and other public-domain items for reproduction.

Local newspapers may sell reproducible photos that were taken by the staff for news stories. These photos may depict celebrities or political figures, or they may show sunsets, riots, fires, traffic accidents, snow-storms, and other news events. If they've only been seen locally, consider them for other projects.

A natural-history museum in town may have a photo collection showing the area's flowers and insects. A school of fashion might let you use photos of their student models.

Don't forget to tap local manufacturers, hospitals, theater groups, restaurants, libraries, museums, collectors' clubs, zoos, and other organizations listed in the local Yellow Pages.

To identify picture agencies and photographers in your area, check the Yellow Pages and the geographic section of the *Directory of Special Libraries and Information Centers*, the *Official Museum Directory*, and the *Stock Photo and Assignment Source Book* mentioned in this chapter. Also, some libraries own a directory of picture sources in their community. They'll help you find picture sources you might have overlooked.

Nationwide directories

If you can't find what you need locally, check nationwide directories. The list below tells you who collects visual material for reproduction.

Public institutions: libraries, museums, historical societies. Public institutions own different amounts of pictorial material. You'll find many varied collections through the directories below.

1. *Contemporary Photographers (CP)*. St. Martin's Press. 1983.

Some books are illustrated with the photos of well-known photographers. *CP*, a who's who of internationally known photographers, names the museums and libraries that own their work. Many photos are available for reproduction. (See also *Index to American Photographic Collections*.)

2. *Directory of Special Libraries and Information Centers*. 5 vols. Gale Research Co. Issued every two years.

This directory identifies special libraries nationwide—for example, art, media, company, hospital, and law libraries. Not every library listed owns pictorial material, and the pictorial holdings that are in special libraries are not necessarily well described in this reference.

Start with the subject index. It includes both broad topics (THEATER) and specific ones (WHISTLER, JAMES ABBOTT MCNEILL).

3. *Guide to the Special Collections of Prints and Photographs in the Library of Congress*, compiled by Paul Vanderbilt. Library of Congress. 1955.

This guide lists 802 collections in the Prints and Photographic Division of the Library of Congress as of 1955. The guide is arranged alphabetically by collection name. For example, you'll read that the Gurrey Collection consists of approximately forty-five photoprints of young adults of mixed racial descent in Hawaii in 1909. Start with the subject index.

4. *Index to American Photographic Collections (IAPC)* compiled at the International Museum of Photography at George Eastman House, edited by James McQuaid. G. K. Hall & Co. 1982.

IAPC lists 458 private and public collections of photographs by some 19,000 nineteenth- and twentieth-century photographers which are owned by historical societies, galleries, museums, libraries, government agencies, universities, etc.

The directory is arranged by state. If you know the precise photographer you're looking for, check the photographer index.

5. *Index to Reproductions of American Paintings* by Isabel Stevenson Monro and Kate M. Monro. H. W. Wilson. 1948. Supplement, 1964.

6. *Index to Reproductions of American Paintings* by Lyn Wall Smith and Nancy Dustin Wall Moure. Scarecrow Press. 1977.

7. *Index to Reproductions of European Paintings* by Isabel Stevenson Monro and Kate M. Monro. H. W. Wilson. 1959.

You may want to use reproductions of paintings to illustrate your work. These guides will tell you which foreign or American museum holds a particular painting so you can order prints. You can check by artist, title, or subject.

Whether you want an artistic representation of something specific, like one of the presidents or Mount Fuji, or an intangible, like a facial expression, you may want to see the painting first. Each index lists hundreds of books that include them, for a preview look.

8. *Official Museum Directory (OMD)*. American Association of Museums. 1973-date. Annual.

Many museums sell or lease photographs related to their collecting specialty. *OMD* lists museums of art, history, and science; historic houses; historical societies; aquariums; botanical gardens; herbariums; planetariums; zoos; national parks, etc. Perhaps the Emmett Kelly Historical Museum of Sedan, Kansas, will have exactly what you need for your circus article.

9. *Sculpture Index (SI)* by Jane Clapp. 4 vols. Scarecrow Press. 1970.

SI is an artist, subject, and title index to sculptures in several thousand American and foreign museums. It also lists more than 925 books that reproduce pictures of them.

10. *Subject Collections* by Lee Ash. R. R. Bowker & Co. Published approximately every five to seven years.

Ash lists special collections by subject in varied libraries. Most of these collections own some pictorial material, although entries give only general information. For example, under CONDUCTORS & CONDUCTING you'll find the Philip Kahgan collection at the University of California, Los Angeles, which contains music, letters, programs, and photographs of the Southern California classical musical scene.

Contact each institution for further information.

Businesses. Many corporations, manufacturers, hospitals, and other businesses keep printed and photographic records of their activities. Often, they're available free or at low cost to writers. If you want a picture of major hotels in Yellowstone National Park or a hot dog-shaped diner in New Jersey, contact them.

Start locally, then check *Directory of Directories (DOD)* for nationwide directories. If your article for a boating magazine demands a picture, *Sailboat & Equipment Directory* might put you in touch with a sailboat maker who has photographs of that product.

The names of other directories listed in *DOD* might suggest other picture sources: *Directory of Fish Culturists, Funparks Directory, Iowa Hay Directory, Turkey World, Leather Manufacturer Directory, U.S. Directory of Meat Slaughtering Plants,* and *Yellow Book of Funeral Directors and Services.*

Societies, associations, clubs. Many professional, trade, and hobby groups collect visual material relating to their interest and activities, whether it's dollhouses, antique cars, or racehorses. Their collections vary from home photographs taken by an officer to a large and carefully maintained archive. A directory of these groups is listed below.

Approach the smaller organizations only when you have time to gather your photos. Many groups are not staffed to fill requests, and their photographs may not be of reproducible quality.

Encyclopedia of Associations (EA) Gale Research Co. Annual.

EA lists some 17,000 associations. Check entries for clues on the extent of pictorial material each group owns. Organizations do not uniformly list the availability of photographs in this source.

A group such as the American Burn Association may lead you to professionals with pictorial material of burn patients. The National Cowboy Hall of Fame and Western Heritage Center may include photographs in its large special library.

Focus on groups that have a staff and a central headquarters rather than groups without them.

Tourist boards, chambers of commerce, embassies. Most cities, states, and countries maintain chambers of commerce, tourist boards, and embassies that strive to promote tourism and attract business to their area. They're usually happy to supply photos, often free of charge. Beware of publicity photos, however, since they're usually cosmetic. The following directories will help you find them.

1. *Encyclopedia of Associations.* Gale Research Co. Annual. (See entry above.)

2. *1,001 Sources for Free Travel Information.* Travel Information Bureau. 1983.

This source names 1,200 tourist-information bureaus, embassies, consulates, United Nations missions, airlines, railroads, chambers of commerce, state development offices, hotel chains, and other sources of travel information in foreign countries and the United States. Arranged geographically.

3. *World Wide Chamber of Commerce Directory.* Johnson Publishing Co. Annual.

Lists chambers of commerce contacts in approximately 7,750 American cities and 275 foreign countries.

4. *Foreign Consular Offices in the United States.* Government Printing Office. Annual.

Arranges, in geographical order, foreign consulates in the United States.

Press agencies and newspapers. Local newspapers cover local news. Press agencies such as United Press International cover the national and international scene. They often sell their photographs for reproduction. Check the following sources for addresses:

1. *Ayer Directory of Publications.* Ayer Press. Annual.

2. *Working Press of the Nation.* National Research Bureau. Annual.

3. *Editor & Publisher International Year Book.* Editor & Publisher, Inc. Annual.

4. *News Bureaus in the U. S.* Public Relations Publishing Co. Biennial, odd years.

Government agencies. Many city, state, and federal agencies that oversee transportation, labor, health, environment, and other services own collections of photographs documenting their activities. For example, the U.S. Bureau of Land Management has more than 22,000 photos of minerals, wildlife, recreation, forests, 1880s land rushes, fire fighting, etc. in Alaska and the Western states. A state department of transportation may own photographs of scenic views, highway construction, state recreational facilities, and bridges. The following directories will guide you to the appropriate government agencies.

1. *Pictorial Resources in the Washington D. C. Area,* compiled by Shirley L. Green. Library of Congress. 1976.

This directory outlines the picture resources of government agencies and also private and international organizations in the District of Columbia, such as the Association of American Railroads and the Pan American Health Organization.

2. *Free Stock Photography Directory.* Infosource Business Publications. 1979.

Lists over 260 federal, state, and local government offices and some corporations that offer free photos for commercial use. The directory provides geographical and subject indexes.

Stock photo agencies. Stock photo agencies are commercial firms that buy photographs from many photographers. They often specialize in certain subjects and, as a result, they can offer comprehensive picture coverage in those fields. Shashinka Photos in New York, for example, has more than 100,000 pictures focussing on East Asian cultures.

There are about 150 stock photos agencies nationwide centered mostly in large cities. Their photos lease from $10 and up.

Stock photo directories include the following:

1. *Art in Life* by Jane Clapp. Scarecrow. 1959. Supplement, 1965.

This is a subject index to the pictures that appeared in *Life* magazine between 1936 and 1963. Most pictures are owned by the magazine, and many are available for lease from Time, Inc.'s Life Picture Service in New York City.

2. *Illustration Index (II).* 1st-5th ed. Scarecrow Press. 1957-84.

II indexes the illustrations that have appeared in such magazines as *American Heritage, Ebony, Holiday, National Geographic, National Wildlife, Natural History, Smithsonian,* and *Sports Illustrated* between 1950 and 1981. Reproduction rights of many of the pictures are available for lease through the magazines listed.

For other listings of stock photo agencies, check *Literary Market Place* (R. R. Bowker & Co.) and *Photographer's Market* (Writer's Digest Books). Agencies are arranged alphabetically with no subject access, so each entry must be examined for the subject you need.

Miscellaneous sources. The following directories list pictures in the public domain. Others include many of the individual picture providers named above.

1. *Hart Picture Archives Series.* Hart Publishing Co.

This is a series of over fifteen books published 1976-date, each reproducing cartoons, drawings, sketches, and engravings from books and magazines in the public domain.

Some volumes in the series are: *European Designs; Oriental Designs; Ships, Seas, and Sailors; Holidays; Borders and Frames; The Animal Kingdom; Humor, Wit, and Fantasy; Jewelry; Chairs; Weather; Dining and Drinking; Faces; Weapons and Armor; Jars, Bowls, and Vases; and Merchandise.*

2. *Picture Sources* by Ann Novotny. 3d ed. Special Libraries Association. 1975.

3. *Stock Photo and Assignment Source Book: Where to Find Photographs Instantly,* edited by Fred W. McDarrah. R. R. Bowker & Co. 1977.

4. *Writer's Resource Guide,* edited by Bernadine Clark. 2d ed. Writer's Digest Books. 1983.

Each directory mentions picture collections in public libraries, state agencies, museums, universities, newspapers, etc. Check subject indexes to find appropriate material.

PRACTICAL CONSIDERATIONS

The directories mentioned in this chapter will help you pinpoint picture sources. All picture sources, however, are not equal.

Libraries, museums, and historical societies, for example, are not in the picture business. Their primary function is to collect and preserve pictures. Leasing them is a secondary function. For this reason, their picture collections are not always well organized. Their pictures may even be mixed with collections of manuscripts and books. Even if the picture collections *are* separate, the pictures may not be cataloged or itemized. The Library of Congress is a case in point. The nine million prints, negatives, slides, and photographs in the Prints & Photographics Division are largely uncataloged and consequently little used. Unless you can identify a specific item in the collection, it's unlikely that you'll get it without an in-person visit.

If a picture collection is small enough, a staff member may photocopy some pictures to help you make a decision. If not, you're out of luck.

Service and fees

When you lease pictures for reproduction, the agency provides you with a print copy, *if* there are extras on hand. Public institutions may not keep extras. To make one, they must have the picture photographed to provide a negative from which prints are then made. This plays havoc with quick service and may not justify the low cost in your situation.

Stock photo agencies, some zoos, newspapers, and other for-profit or public relations-minded organizations usually offer the quickest service. Providing prints is part of their business, if not their entire business. So, they keep prints on hand. Even if a stock photo agency charges you between $10 and $100 for a one-time use of a picture, it may still be cheaper than a library's $5 or $10 charge if you consider your time.

Your fee is based on how a picture is ultimately used. Pictures used in articles usually lease for a lower fee than pictures used in books. Furthermore, the larger the press run of a book, the higher the fee. There is still another fee schedule if the picture is to be used in advertising.

If fast service is your major concern, use a commercial source.

Copyrights and permissions. Organizations that lease their photographs include in their leasing agreement the conditions under which a photo can be used. The lender will also specify that you not make extra copies for reuse after you return the print because you bought one-time use rights only.

If you take your own photographs and intend to sell them, the issue of copyright becomes crucial. You must know, for example, that you may need permission to photograph a famous work of art. Even if you get it, you may not be able to reproduce your photograph. What about the problems involved with publishing photographs of public figures or private individuals? To identify the most recent books on photography and copyright, check *Subject Guide to Books in Print* under PHOTOGRAPHY—LAW AND LEGISLATION.

There's little question that illustrations are an important part of reading matter today. By acquainting ourselves with the sources of pictures, we can increase our chances of a sale.

18
FINDING AND CONTACTING EXPERTS

Most writing projects demand some input from an expert, whether it's a coin collector you're interviewing for an article or a librarian you're asking for general research help.

Finding such experts as contractors, jewelers, or child psychologists may be as easy as checking your local phone book. Less-visible experts—someone who raises African violets, won a blue ribbon at a fair, or lived in Alaska before 1970—may be found through the grapevine: a club, business, museum, church, university, store, or organization connected with their unique interest or skill.

Another way to locate hard-to-find experts is to check a nationwide directory. *Directory of Directories (DOD)*, mentions thousands—*Major Oil Spill Directory, Directory of Wire Companies of North America, Annual Directory of Religious Broadcasting, Shooting Industry Buyers Guide*, etc.

Encyclopedia of Associations (EA) is another source of experts. For a special question about Mongolians, contact the Mongolia Society. For firsthand information on science education in China, try the Chinese Institute of Engineers—USA. Associations listed in *EA* are varied, ranging from the Center for Attitudinal Healing, a group advocating spiritual psychotherapy for people with life-threatening diseases, to the Chile Legislative Center, a human-rights group.

Nationwide directories are sometimes very effective in pinpointing experts in your own backyard. Many nationwide associations, for example, can direct you to local chapters not listed in the phone book. To find African violet growers, as mentioned in the beginning of this chapter, check with the African Violet Society of America, listed in *EA*; to identify someone who won a blue ribbon at a fair, you might contact the National 4-H Council. And *EA* names a group called Alaska Yukon Pioneers, which no doubt includes people who lived in Alaska before 1970.

The National Referral Center (NRC) at the Library of Congress in Washington, D.C. (20540) is useful for writers who don't have access to *EA* or *DOD*. At least one of the 13,000 organizations in the NRC file doubtless deals with your topic.

When you contact associations, you may find them remarkably receptive to helping you. They often send writers a list of recommended readings, their newsletter or magazine, and photocopies of pertinent magazine articles written by or about them.

Many of the directories and reference books mentioned in previous chapters are also useful in locating experts. This includes current biographical directories such as *Who's Who in Engineering* or *Who's Who in the Theatre.*

Books on special subjects—hydroponic gardening or corporate espionage—can also lead you to experts. Many books are written, not by full-time writers, but by experts in some field. Joseph McNamara, the police chief of San Jose, California, wrote *Safe and Sane,* a guide to protecting yourself and your property; former Internal Revenue Service agent Randy Blaustein wrote *How to Do Business with the IRS.* This research book you're reading now was written by a librarian. Some author might be the very expert you're looking for.

CONTACTING EXPERTS

Now that you've found the expert or special source of information you need, how do you make contact?

A book like *The Craft of Interviewing* by John Brady can give you many pointers on how to reach people successfully, whether you go through channels or bypass them. Articles in writers' magazines also give useful tips that free-lancers have developed to reach people quickly. They may range from something as simple as enclosing a self-addressed stamped envelope in a letter to psychological ploys such as sounding urgent when you call. What I've discovered to work best is to make it as easy as possible for a person to respond to your query.

Getting information from people can be frustrating. Perhaps you'll call for an appointment and instead, you find that the person or organization is shielded by a wall of secretaries. You'll undoubtedly get cut off during long-distance calls, too, or put on hold. Letters sometimes come back for one reason or another, and you have to start all over. Or the person you wrote to doesn't respond.

These occurrences are normal. You can't fight them. You can, however, develop a strategy that will increase your chances of success.

If you decide to call

What if you've made several calls to someone who doesn't return them? There are several reasons why people don't return phone calls. The person may have been on a rush job or out of the office repeatedly. No response can also mean "no" or "I can't help you." Some people get so many requests that responding even with negative answers is time consuming. So they only respond to calls from people they *can* help.

Often, busy people who don't return calls like to be called back. A person may have every intention of answering your letter but just not have a spare moment. You're not likely to get a letter telling you why it's taking so long.

If your need is urgent, call the person. It sometimes gives him or her a chance to get added information you might have overlooked in your letter. In the end, a phone call from you may make it easy for that person to respond.

If you decide to write

Sometimes a person or organization wants your question in writing. This has advantages. It puts your request in a tangible form the person can refer to.

Communicating effectively, however, regardless of the medium, requires skill. There are ways to request information by mail that will encourage a response and restore some of the control you've lost by having to depend on someone far away. (Many of the tips below also apply to requests you make by phone.)

Legibility. Write clearly. *You* may be able to read your own handwriting but others may not. If you can, type your letters. Letters that can't be read can't be answered.

Sentence length and clarity. Keep your sentences brief but clear. Many people write as they speak, complete with long, rambling sentences. A style like this can hide your question.

Spelling and grammar. Nothing looks worse than a letter that buzzes with bad grammar and misspelled words, especially in an article query or book proposal. It will do more harm to your request than you can measure.

Be aware of the tone of your request. Politeness still counts. Remember this when you lose your cool. Everyone has feelings. Offended people find it very easy to put off those who give them a hard time.

A positive and polite approach will keep the doors to cooperation wide open. Even if the person can't help you this time, you may need a favor another time.

Know what you want. If you ask a broad or general question, not only do you make your letter difficult to answer, you also signal that you probably don't know what you really want. When a woman asked me for a nationwide list of firms that do dyeing work, I asked her three or four questions more. Dyeing of what? Carpeting? Drapes? Leather? Shoes? Upholstery? For industrial purposes or for individuals? If there's no directory that says it all, this kind of question becomes impossible to answer.

Learn how to ask for information. Follow the general instructions in chapter 5 on how to ask a question. The same rules apply for letters as for in-person requests. Tell the person what you're doing and why. Be specific. Don't say "recently" if you mean ten years ago. A clerk searching through sixty years of files must be able to narrow the period searched if the files are not all-in-one. If the task is too time-consuming without that vital piece of information, the clerk won't be able to help you.

How much should you ask? Are you asking one question in a letter or ten? Each additional question that must be researched slows down the entire query.

Perhaps a response to your request can't be comfortably handled by a letter. Many busy people don't have the time to write their life stories in 250 words or less or expound on their opinions of military rule in Latin America. In your query, you might offer the expert the option of responding either by phone or by letter. The easier the response, the likelier you are to receive it.

Do your homework. Before you start contacting experts, bone up on your subject. This will help you formulate questions you want to ask. In any event, busy people will appreciate your consideration of their time if you avoid asking fundamentals you could have gotten from a book.

Start close to home. Check local sources first. It's not always necessary to contact someone halfway around the world. The answer may be within walking or driving distance.

I write a newspaper column, and out-of-state visitors who pick up the paper often write me when they return home for information they could easily get from their public libraries. Why wait up to six months querying someone hundreds of miles away when you can easily get help in ten minutes with a local phone call?

Ask about costs involved in filling your request. Whether you write or call for information, you may have to pay for photocopying or other services. An expert may not charge you for a reprint of an article, but some organizations charge nominal sums to cover their expenses. Most organizations will not fill orders without first notifying you of the costs, but occasionally someone forgets. Many writers include a check with instructions to fill the request up to the amount of the check. This can help save an additional letter.

Enclose a self-addressed stamped envelope. Whether or not the organization is large and can afford a stamp is not the point. It's one of those little things that makes it easier for a busy individual within the organization to respond.

Note your deadline. Mention your deadline if you have one. A busy person would rather know you have one than take valuable time to provide information that won't be used beyond a certain date.

Start well in advance of your deadline. Give yourself enough time for things to go wrong. People are invariably not in when you call the first time. By the time you link up, a week may have passed. That's when you discover you were calling the wrong person.

If things go smoothly and you've arranged an interview well ahead of schedule, you should remind the person close to the interview date.

Addressing the envelope. Have you made sure the address you're using is correct and you haven't transposed any numbers on the envelope?

If you're writing to a large organization or business, you must include a person's name or at least the correct department in the address. Large organizations receive their mail through a central mail room where clerks sort and distribute it. Letters addressed to the organization in general must be opened and screened once more before they get to the right person—*if* they get to the right person. With no name or department on the envelope, you're depending on a mail clerk or secretary to make that decision for you. If they make it incorrectly, your letter can be delayed or lost.

My favorite time-saver is not to mention a person's name on the envelope but to mention the purpose of the letter in the lower left corner of the envelope. For example: "RE: request for a birth certificate copy" or "CONTENTS; proposal and outline for a young adult nonfiction science book." This usually gets your query to the right department and the appropriate person as quickly as a specific name.

Follow-up. If you send a follow-up letter to an unanswered mail or phone request, include the date of the original request and summarize the question. This will help if the first letter was never received. Also, people in large organizations handle many requests. They don't recall every letter they got in the past few months, nor do they always have time to hunt it down to find out what you asked. This is another of those efforts on your part that makes it easier for someone to answer your letter.

Don't forget to say thanks. There's no better way to make a friend than by showing appreciation for a person's efforts, especially when special expertise or time was invested. Besides, you never know when you may need help from that person or organization again.

Each information request presents different problems that must be handled. Common sense and experience should be your guide.

19
SAMPLE SEARCHES

Throughout the book I've stressed that research, regardless of the subject, follows a pattern. For most projects, the seven steps below will uncover more information than you imagined existed.

1. Magazine and newspaper articles

2. Books

3. Encyclopedias

4. Reference books

5. Government documents

6. Original material (private papers, public records, etc.)

7. Experts and organizations

The number of steps you ultimately use and the order in which you use them are not inviolable. Feel free to add or change any to suit your particular project. By following a systematic approach as suggested by this framework, you'll be certain to cover most bases regardless of your project's subject. If you should skip a step, you'll have other chances to find the information, since the same material tends to show up in many resources.

The sample searches that follow will show you how to use the seven steps in two kinds of writing projects—a book and an article.

SAMPLE SEARCH NO. 1: A HISTORICAL NOVEL

This hypothetical novel is set in Massachusetts in the early nineteenth century. Let's say you already have your characters and plot in mind. Now you want to research the plight of the poor in that era and learn more about the setting and customs of the period and place.

Step 1: magazine and newspaper articles

Two useful indexes to check are *Poole's Index* (1802-1906) and *Writings on American History (WAH)* or *America: History and Life*.

Poole's will give you information on issues of the day in such magazines as *Good Works* and *Knickerbocker* magazine. You may find useful articles under the subject POOR, for example and its many subdivisions.

POOR
>—Condition of.
>—Education of.
>—Employment for.
>—How to relieve.

Check other subject headings, too, such as MARRIAGE, LABOR, or even BERKSHIRE MOUNTAINS and any others on which you need information.

If the library you use owns a microform set of magazines entitled *American Periodicals, 1741-1900*, you'll be able to read the articles you find through *Poole's* in microform. Otherwise, you can get the articles through interlibrary loan.

WAH indexes articles in history magazines that might enrich your book in ways you hadn't imagined. For example, consider the following articles from the 1949 issue of *WAH* listed under the heading MASSACHUSETTS:

> "When Massachusetts played the lottery" [1687-1833]. *New England Quarterly*, vol. 22, pp. 316-22, 1949.
> "History of Boston's water supply," 1652-1940. *Bostonian Society Proceedings*, 1948.
> "Did labor support Jackson? The Boston story" [1828-36]. *Political Science Quarterly*, vol. 64, 1949.
> "When Boston Harbor Froze" [Feb. 1844]. *Old-time New England*, vol. 39, 1949.

Old newspapers on microfilm will help you establish your novel's atmosphere and fill it with important background facts. Check local libraries for a microform set of newspapers entitled *Early American Newspapers, 1704-1820*. If no library near you owns it, check the reference book *Newspapers in Microform, 1948-1972* to identify old Massachusetts tabloids which have been microfilmed, such as the *Boston Patriot and Daily Mercantile Advertiser*, which ran from 1819 to 1824, or the *Salem Gazette*, published from 1790 to 1908. These may be available through your library's interlibrary loan service.

Step 2: books

Subject Guide to Books in Print (SGBIP) will identify many useful books. Perhaps you want to know about seeing-eye dogs (*"Guide Dogs for the Blind"*), everyday life in the early nineteenth century (*"Life in America One Hundred Years Ago,"* reprint of the 1914 edition), means of transportation used in the period (*"The Transportation Revolution, 1815-1860"*) or the history of a Massachusetts city (*"The History of Hadley, Massachusetts,"* reprint of the 1905 edition.) If one of your female characters is Jewish, *"The American Jewish Woman, 1654-1980"* should help you make this character more realistic.

Books on cookery, etiquette, customs and manners, etc. will show you how your historical characters should look and behave. Reprinted diaries will offer insights on their thoughts and speech.

Don't forget to watch for bibliographies listing articles and out-of-print books. For example, a costume bibliography might help you identify readings on everything from colonial dress to military uniforms throughout the ages.

Collections of books in microform will uncover old books many libraries do not own. The *Library of American Civilization* set, owned by many large libraries, is the easiest to use because of its useful printed indexes.

Step 3: encyclopedias

Articles on various states and cities in old encyclopedias such as *New American Cyclopaedia* (1861) give details on everything from a city's population to the salaries of local officials. Other articles, such as MORTGAGE, OBSTETRICS (MIDWIVERY), or UNIVERSITIES, will give you more nineteenth-century insights and data.

Step 4: reference books

Reference books can help you do everything from verify the date a historic treaty was signed to identifying names popular in the nineteenth century.

For example, the *Atlas of American History* will reveal, through maps, such information as railroad lines, canals, and military forts that existed in various periods and places.

A *Field Guide to American Houses* can show you housing styles in different parts of the country during different periods; the *Statistical Abstract of the United States* can tell you the outcome of early nineteenth-century presidential elections, the number of votes cast, and the population by state and decade, among other things.

Step 5: government documents

Documents may help you establish certain facts that are difficult to find in other resources. The *Serial Set*, for example, indexes such House and Senate documents as "Citizens of Boston asking relief from deranged state of currency" and "Memorial of inhabitants of Boston for discontinuance of Sabbath mails." Some documents you'll use will be as short as one page; others are book length.

Step 6: primary sources

Many novels and nonfiction books have evolved from real-life diaries and correspondence. Check historical societies and directories of special collections through the directories mentioned in chapter 2. For example, the Shaker collection in the Fruitlands Museum in Harvard, Massachusetts, contains correspondence, diaries, account books, church records, even recipes and scrapbooks from the Shaker communities in Harvard and Shirley, Massachusetts, between 1790-1911. You might find such a special collection of materials near you.

Step 7: experts and organizations

Check *Encyclopedia of Associations*, Lee Ash's *Subject Collections*, or *Official Museum Directory* to identify a special association, collection, or museum with materials on a specific aspect of your topic. Examples include Friends of Historical Pharmacy; the special collection of publications on the occult (black magic, witchcraft, demonology, etc.) at the Los Angeles Public Library; or the Rosicrucian Planetarium and Science Museum in San Jose, with its collection of astronomy and astromythology materials.

SAMPLE SEARCH NO. 2: AN ARTICLE

Let's say you want to write an article on women and stress. You initially want to determine if there are differences in how men and women handle stress. Otherwise, you're not sure of your precise focus at this point.

Step 1: magazine and newspaper articles

First, you must do some market research. *Magazine Index (MI)* will identify articles that have run in paying markets. The April, 1984, issue of *Essence* magazine features an article on stress in black women. An article in the August, 1984, issue of *Working Woman* tells women how to manage job stress. After scanning the complete list in *MI*, you might start to further refine your focus and even think of specific markets. Perhaps you'll want to write on stress and the new mother or stress and the widow.

Your actual research will take you to new indexes, such as *Index Medicus*, *Women Studies Abstracts*, or *Social Sciences Index*. *SSI*, for example, includes some articles on sex differences in stress response:

> Sex differences in psychological distress among married people. P. D. Cleary and D. Mechanic. *Journal of Health and Social Behavior*, vol. 24, pp. 111-21. June 1983.
>
> Sex differences in vulnerability to undesirable life events. *American Sociological Review*. vol. 49, p. 620-31, Oct. 1984.

The *National Newspaper Index* on microfilm, covering five major newspapers, supplements the information you'll find in periodical indexes. For example, you'll find an article in the August 8, 1985, issue of *The New York Times* entitled "Women and Stress: Is Problem Worse at Home or on Job?"

Step 2: books

Subject Guide to Books in Print lists many books on stress. One that looks useful is *Women in Stress: The Nursing Perspective* by Diane Kjervik and Ida Martinson. Or, you might want to start with a bibliography, such as *Physiology of Physical Stress: A Selective Bibliography, 1500-1964* compiled by Carleton Chapman and Elinor Reinmiller.

Step 3: encyclopedias

You'll find a long article on stress in the twelve-volume *International*

Encyclopedia of Psychiatry, Psychology, Psychoanalysis and Neurology which includes a brief section on gender. This may give you some technical insights on sex differences in response to stress.

Step 4: reference books

This step doesn't help in this search. In any event, much of the information that might appear in random reference books shows up through the other steps.

Step 5: government documents

Recent items listed in *Publications Reference File* and *Index to U.S. Government Periodicals* cover stress in hospital patients, the police, the military, and children, though nothing at the moment that focuses on women and stress. A government-published bibliography entitled *Coping and Adaptation: An Annotated Bibliography and Study Guide,* by George Coelho and Richard Irving, may be useful in uncovering hidden material in other documents.

Step 6: primary sources

This step does not appear applicable in this search.

Step 7: experts and organizations

Is there a stress specialist to contact for an interview? Have you investigated any of the author/specialists who wrote any of the articles you found in scholarly magazines? *Encyclopedia of Associations* will also lead you to pertinent individuals through groups such as the American Institute of Stress and the Academy of Stress and Chronic Diseases.

These sample searches should demonstrate that you can research diverse topics by following the same steps. You'll be amazed at the amount of material you find, too. If the steps don't reveal much, you'll at least know you've tried almost everything. At the same time, you may have found a new book topic that's never been done.

Index

ABOUT THE AUTHOR

As a reference librarian at the University of California-San Diego for eight years and through her thrice-weekly column, "The Reference Librarian," for *The San Diego Union*, Lois Horowitz has helped thousands of people from all walks of life find information on everything from the care and feeding of pet guppies to how to trace a missing person. Her goal is not just to dispense information—it's to supply writers with the tools they need for digging out the facts that make books and articles sparkle.

She has also put her research skills and methods to good use as a freelance writer. Her articles have appeared in such publications as *Nutshell*, *Family Health*, and *Writer's Digest*, and she is the former book critic for *The San Diego Tribune*.